# NEVER DIE YOUNG

ROBERT WILLIAM HULT

Copyright © 2019 by Robert William Hult.

ISBN    Softcover    978-1-951469-67-2

Cover: The Thinker by French sculptor, Auguste Rodin

All rights reserved. No part of this book may be reproduced or transmitted in any form or by any means, electronic or mechanical, including photocopying, recording, or by any information storage and retrieval system without express written permission from the author, except in the case of brief quotations embodied in critical reviews and certain other non-commercial uses permitted by copyright law.

Printed in the United States of America.

To order additional copies of this book, contact:
**Bookwhip**
1-855-339-3589
https://www.bookwhip.com

*For those still growing . . .*

# Contents

Prologue ..................................................................................1
Nearly Dead at Birth ................................................................3
Brown Bear Attack ...................................................................4
Chasing Girls ............................................................................7
King of the Mountain ...............................................................9
Almost Drowned by a Catfish ................................................11
Twelve-Year-Old Runaway .....................................................13
Grizzly Bear Attack .................................................................17
Low Self Esteem .....................................................................20
Escaping an Elk ......................................................................23
Hypothermia ..........................................................................26
Gymnastics .............................................................................31
The Tower ..............................................................................34
Manana Island and Turtle Island ...........................................40
Sudden Death on a Busy Freeway ..........................................46
Alcohol Poisoning ..................................................................49
Submarine Sounding .............................................................51
One Cold January Morning ...................................................54
Skana, a Killer Whale .............................................................58
Packrats and Rattlesnakes ......................................................62
Staking Mineral Rights ..........................................................66
Disassembling an Antique Barn .............................................69
Climbing Silver Star ...............................................................73
Dead Man's Canyon ...............................................................76
The Executive Monkey ...........................................................83
Building a Home ....................................................................92
Falls ......................................................................................103
Epilogue ...............................................................................105

At four years old, I loved horses and
I could ride proficiently.

# Prologue

My father led a hard life and died at 49; he should have lived for another 50 years. My youngest brother committed suicide. I had seen him two weeks earlier and had no idea of the stress he was under. Around me, he was always upbeat. He should have lived another 50 or so years as well.

I was going to write this book for my family, but now, looking at my life and the lives of my father and youngest brother, I feel I have some things to share with young people—ideas about life, living, and just trying to be happy.

All of us, at one time or another, have wondered why we are here. The answers range from the truly mundane to the spiritual. My 70ish-year history on this planet has been fraught with misadventures, accidents and miscalculations. I have been on the brink of death several times. From time to time, I have had to ask myself, "Why am I still here, and others I knew aren't?"

There are those who say, "What doesn't kill you, makes you stronger." After my own near-death experiences, I think so, too. The stories in this little book are a part of an autobiography, a personal journey, reflections from experience. These stories actually happened. You will read them pretty much in chronological order as they happened.

Mine seemed like a pretty insignificant life. It certainly wasn't boring, however. After you read about these many odd adventures and misadventures, you will probably brush the sweat off on your brow and say, as I often have, "How did one survive that?" Good parents will always tell you that there are consequences to your actions. These stories prove it.

The major part of the audience of these stories I believe ought to be young people, who are just beginning the most interesting parts of their lives. I hope these true stories help to create some awareness of impending disaster and potential doom if one goes about life willy-nilly without thinking things through. I have discovered that even if one prepares oneself for most every eventuality, certain terrible things can happen anyway. I know that because they happened to me, and I gained some insight because of them. I believe you will, too.

For a naturally curious person, our world is full of challenges. There is no end of things to see and do, and some of these things are downright dangerous. Often, especially for a young person, the challenges are irresistible, despite the fact there are hidden hazards. When one is young and bubbling with energy, one often does not appreciate or respect the problems nature has created while evolving something awesome.

Around the corner or under the surface, there can always be something a human being will not expect, and what that is may not be life threatening to other animals, but to a person with our limited sense knowledge and mobility, it could be deadly.

In my long life, I have come across some of these hazards, which have challenged my personal best. Again, these are real stories, gleaned from past encounters with nature and with her wildlife. I have learned valuable lessons from each of these situations. Some of them I would not care to repeat; others I would do over, only because I now have the experience to deal with the challenges they presented to me.

From reading these episodes, I hope you come away with an appreciation of nature's challenges and what it takes to live through some of them.

People die every day from unexpected consequences. To only be prepared is not enough to survive. Sometimes a person needs to draw from very deep inside themselves.

# Nearly Dead at Birth

In 1947, having jaundice at birth was a serious, life-threatening malady. Neither was my head a normal shape when it came out the birth canal. For both reasons, doctors feared I might have a life-ending disability, and at any rate, it would take years and years of nearly constant massage by my parents to create a normal looking head. That mostly happened.

Perhaps, that's why I have always had so much empathy throughout my life for other people with disabilities of one kind or another. I could have easily been any one of those people, that I cared so much for later in life.

For me, life has been full of such circles.

To take care of the yellow jaundice, my doctors gave me a complete blood transfusion from the blood of another person. I am a Type 0 so I can give freely to others and thank God type O positive is a common blood type, so I was able to easily access someone else's blood. Thank you to whoever that was or I probably would not be writing this. Sixty-five years later, I received another complete blood transfusion for a different kind of life-saving situation. I daily thank whoever supplied that blood as well, or I would not be walking. Rather, I would have been in a wheel-chair the rest of my life as was my Italian grandmother on my mother's side of the family.

# Brown Bear Attack

It is always a good idea to be wary of large carnivorous animals and even at four years of age, no-one had to teach me that.

At the time, my mother and father and I lived on Kodiak Mountain, near the Kodiak Island Naval Air Station. My father's job as an air traffic control man took us there for four years. My younger brother, Stephen, was born on Kodiak Island and he has always had a yen to go back.

I went to school at the base kindergarden and graduated to first grade there. One of my favorite activities was to ride in my father's jeep that he took to work every day. My father's favorite activity was to fish for huge salmon that ran up Kodiak's largest river.

We went fishing every chance he was off duty and whenever the salmon were running. Now, Kodiak Island was known in 1951 as having 3,000 Kodiak natives, 3,000 naval personnel and 1,000 Kodiak brown bears, a kind of grizzly bear that had adapted itself to Kodiak Island over the centuries. These bears weren't afraid of anything or anybody. If you were fishing for salmon, so were they.

As I recall, it was a beautiful fall day and the salmon were thick in the river. Fishermen were up and down the river up to their kneecaps in their rubber waders. It had been about an hour before dad caught his salmon. When he finally got it to shore, it was huge, nearly as long as I was tall.

Sometimes we went fishing with my dad's best friend, William, whose name is my middle name. But William was working in the

Kodiak Tower, bringing in and sending out airplanes. It was only me and dad this particular day. As a result, when dad wanted to take a picture of the big fish, it was up to me to hold it off the ground.

The fish weighed nearly as much as I did, and as I said, it was as long as I was tall, so trying to hold it high enough off the ground to get a good picture was quite a challenge for a four-year old. Dad kept urging me to hold it higher . . . to get its wide tail off the ground.

It was about that time that I saw the bear coming across the river. He had spotted me holding the fish up. My father's back was to the approaching bear.

"Daddy, there is a bear coming," I said, softly at first, maybe thinking the big animal couldn't hear me, if I said it soft enough.

"Hold the fish higher, Bobby," said my father, Robert.

I tried. The big bear was halfway through the river and getting nearer.

"There's a bear coming," I said a little louder.

I'm not sure whether my father just didn't hear me behind the fish, or whether he was actually concentrating too hard on the picture with his little black box Kodiak camera.

I held the fish a little higher.

"Come on, now. You're stronger than that. Get its tail off the ground."

I pushed up a little harder and looked around its body.

"A BEAR IS COMING!" I screamed.

The scaggly young bear's head was approaching shore.

Finally, my dad looked around. He saw what was bothering me. The big animal had one paw on land and three in the water.

Without a word, dad dropped the camera, and rushed toward me. He grabbed me by the waist in one hand and the salmon by the gills in the other hand.

We headed at full speed toward the Jeep.

I was looking backward. I could see the waterlogged bear behind us and the salmon's head beside me in dad's other hand as he frantically made his way along the pebble strewn beach toward the road, still several yards away.

At four, I didn't know that bears can run fast. In fact, they can keep up thirty five miles an hour for quite a long time. But this bear had decided he was hungry, and maybe, being a young bear, he wasn't a good salmon fisherman yet. He started to chase us.

Dad looked backward and saw that bear coming faster. I remember being very happen when I saw dad drop that fish. I'm still not sure whether it was just too heavy to carry or if it just slipped out of his other hand.

At any rate, it stopped the bear from getting too close to me and dad. While I was still bouncing up and down, I watched the animal stop and sniff it. Then he took it in his mouth, gave a kind of chuffing sound, and turned around and carried it off.

As dad put me in the passenger side of the Jeep, I saw the wet brown bear take his stolen prize back to the river, presumably to eat it.

We didn't wait around to find out.

# Chasing Girls

Young people are generally so intent on the use of their bodies at an early age, that they rarely see, much less understand that which is going on in the environment around them. So it was for me when I got off a school bus near my home and started chasing a ten-year-old girl I knew. I can't remember why I was chasing her, of course, but the event landed me in a naval hospital. At the time, I was also ten years old.

I was chasing the girl, books under her arm, up a slight up-grade. A large boy on a bicycle was coming down the hill at the same time. We collided. The bicycle and its rider rode right over the top of me. To this day, I can't see through my minds' eye how it happened that I ended up on the paved street and the bicycle was still going down the street, as if nothing had happened. One could call it a "hit and run."

Someone on my block called my mother. When she found me, I was bleeding profusely from a wound on my left waist and from a similarly long cut on the left side of my head. She rushed me to the Sand Point Naval Air Station in Seattle, Washington, and to the only hospital there, the one in which I was born.

The operating room seemed familiar and I was comfortable there under anesthetic. Probably, I was delirious from the loss of blood from my head and from my side. I remember pulling—lots of pulling as the doctor put thirteen stitches into my head and another thirteen into my side.

It was weeks before the same doctor took out the stitches, one at a time. They didn't use staples in those days, just silk thread. If a person did too much strenuous exercise, he could pull out those stitches. My mother tried to keep me in bed a good deal of the time for that very reason.

About the only good that resulted from that accident was that kids from my block and surrounding blocks, who had heard of the incident, came over to my house with bundles of comic books. Before long, I had a stack nearly three feet high that regularly wanted to be two stacks, equally high. Day after day, week after week, I read those comics. Many of them I read twice and three times, which possibly accounts for my still keen fascination with fantasy and why I am good at writing it. However, there was a good lesson: don't chase girls. These days, I don't chase anything.

# King of the Mountain

The first and only house my parent's ever bought together was near Mountlake Terrace, Washington. It was four blocks from Lake Ballinger, a fair-sized lake that had a natural population of fish–some catfish and croppy, but mostly rainbow trout and perch.

One summer, I spent every single day from about eleven o clock to about four in the afternoon fishing. I caught so many fish I couldn't eat them all. My parents let me keep them in our big, round plastic pool in the backyard. Essentially, I had my own personal mini-aquarium and I studied the fish I caught.

It took me awhile, but I figured out what different kinds of fish like to eat. (I'll bet you didn't know that trout like pork and beans.) Insight into fish behavior made me an even better juvenile fisherman. I was eleven years old then. Before that, however, I was pretty good at playing king of the mountain.

One spring day I was playing king of the mountain on a newly built sand mountain that had been constructed by a building company that was ready to place a new building in the neighborhood. There were big rocks and small rocks all over that mountain. The mountain itself was about fifteen feet tall. Six of us boys and one girl were running up and down the mountain, trying to keep others from staying on top. It was a rough and tumble kind of play. We'd push others and they would push us. No one really expected anyone else to get seriously hurt . . . maybe just a bruise or two the next day.

When I got to the top, one of the bigger boys pushed me and I rolled down. I was eager to rejoin my friends, who were still at the top. On my next trip up the mountain, however, someone rolled down one of the big rocks. About half way up the mountain, that boulder connected with my head and knocked me unconscious. And not only that, but it split my skull. Out of a two-inch crevice, blood began gushing out.

Someone called my mother. My father was working at his extra job at Boeing Field as an air traffic controller.

Friends say I was a blooming mess, bloody and sandy from one end to the other. An ambulance came and took me away. By that time, I had lost so much blood, I nearly died.

The next thing I remember, I was in the military hospital again, getting more blood again, and having my head stitched up, again. It took over 20 stitches to put me back together and I still bear the scar from that episode today.

I can imagine my poor mother saying to herself, "Is this what having boys is all about . . . one catastrophe after another?"

So much for being king of the mountain.

# Almost Drowned by a Catfish

Summer arrived and I began fishing. The previous summer I had caught the record catfish in the lake. He was nearly three feet long and it was a pleasure eating him. This summer, I hoped to catch another catfish and eat him, too. So it was I was standing on a dock with my fishing pole, my small tackle box only a few feet away. And yep, I caught another catfish. But this one had a terrible surprise for me.

As I began pulling him up through the green lily pads, he began pulling on me. We had quite the fierce battle for several minutes. Usually pulling in a catfish is like pulling in a small log. In the South, catfish actually fight like trout. They are often caught and eaten, but in the Pacific Northwest, most people don't even try to catch them.

I knew this one was big, maybe even bigger than the previous one and I planted my feet on the dock. As I was reeling him in, just about the time I saw him, he must have seen me, too, because he took off like a rocket. I didn't expect that and I lost my balance as he swept me off my feet, pulling me right into the lake. On the way down, I kicked over my tackle box and it landed in the lake, quickly sinking out of sight.

The real problem for me was . . . I didn't know how to swim. I let loose of the fishing pole and it took off. Before I knew it, the circular current in the lake transported me over twenty feet from the dock and even further from the reed and cattail covered shore.

I guarantee you that if you are in this situation, you will panic. And I did.

I struggled to keep my head above water and started yelling. Unfortunately, there was no-one around to hear my loud distress cries.

When you panic, you tend to keep your hands over your head and that sinks your head below the water. Also, my tennis shoes and jeans and shirt were now waterlogged and they weren't helping my situation, either. I could have easily drowned that day and I'm not exactly sure why I didn't.

All I remember thinking about was that catfish and that if he could still swim with a line and a pole attached to him, I should be able to swim, also.

I remembered the fish in my pool and even in such a tight enclosure, they seemed to have no trouble swimming any direction they pleased.

Instead of flailing around up and down in the same spot and swallowing a lot of water, I decided it was better to be a fish and get my body horizontal. It took me awhile to figure out how to do it, but I was getting very tired and somehow I did it.

I started holding my breath and using my arms to kind of dog-paddle. Low and behold, I started going with the current and my dog-paddling and holding my breath got me to another dock a couple hundred feet away, which I grabbed hold of in desperation.

I yelled some more, but still no-one came to my rescue.

At least now I could get to shore and I struggled with one hand hold over another until I got to shallow water, where I could stand up. I was exhausted and when I got to the lawn that was attached to the dock, I just laid there and caught my breath. Fortunately, it was a nice warm day. I wasn't feeling a bit cold as I walked the four blocks home, thankful to see another afternoon.

Because I was soaking wet when I got home and I had to explain why I had lost my fishing pole and tackle box, I told my mother about the incident. I would definitely need another set of gear and she would be the one who might buy it for me, maybe for mowing the lawn every week for a month.

I said to her, "Guess what, Mother? Today, a catfish taught me how to swim."

# Twelve-Year-Old Runaway

Parents are frantic when their kids are lost or run away from home. There are so many situations a child cannot control once they do run. But there are generally good reasons why a child does run away. I know, because I did it. A person I once knew (deceased now) did it because his father was a religious zealot and wouldn't allow his son to play a musical instrument. His son ran all the way from Boston to San Francisco.

I did it because I had an abusive father.

My father was a mean drunk. When he drank over his limit, which was often, particular when he was stressed out, he would lash out at his sons. By the time I was twelve, there were four boys in my immediate family. Steven was four years younger than me, Mark was six years younger, and David was eight years younger. Fortunately, they didn't have to put up with him for very long. He and my mother divorced.

When I almost thirteen, I could tell my father and mother were already having troubles, both emotionally, financially, and physically. They rarely talked to one another. When they did, they argued.

Part of the problem was my father's job; his was in the high stress world of air traffic control and he first started out in the Navy on board aircraft carriers as an aircraft control technician. He brought down planes from the sky to land on these aircraft carriers, a tricky situation, and I was to learn a tricky job at best. He often brought the stress of his job home with him.

Also, my father grew up in an era, both in the Navy and in his formative years, where gin and whisky alcohol were the drinks of choice. "Have a problem, hit the bottle," seemed to be the motto of his generation. High toxicity whisky was my father's favorite choice.

Now, I didn't necessarily blame him . . . much. He, his mother, and his sister walked away from their family when he was a teenager in Boston. They came to settle out west in Puyallup, Washington.

To make ends meet, his older sister married a man nearly three times her age. When that didn't work out, she jumped off the tall Narrow's Bridge in Tacoma and committed suicide.

I never really knew my Swedish grandmother, Hilda, out of her old folk's home bed where my father supported her until the day she died.

That was the only day I ever saw my father cry. That was the only day I ever saw my mother support my father. After that, everything went downhill. Dad took to drinking in earnest.

I don't remember why my father hit me the first time, but it made quite an impression. Those were the days before child abuse laws in the United States. The second time he hit me caused a huge black eye that I sported for weeks. I made big plans to leave home permanently.

Kids do things that aren't quite rational. It is because their frontal cortex isn't yet developed and in boys this doesn't happen until they are about twenty-one or so. That's of course why boys are not allowed to do certain legal things until they are twenty-one.

But no-one ever explained things like that to me. So: I planned a trip to Anaheim, California; by myself. I planned it for weeks. My idea was to get a job at Disneyland, an interesting idea for a sheltered child who doesn't know the world, doesn't know its hazards, doesn't even know how to get from Washington State to California, or how long it takes by bicycle.

There is only so much stuff one can carry in a packsack on a three-speed bike and I had everything I thought I needed. And, planning a trip from where I lived to California isn't easy when there are four boys living in one room in two bunk beds. Someone is liable to notice you stashing things in a pack sack. But I was cagy about it and the day came when I had everything I thought I needed. I arranged the kitchen and bedroom so that it looked like nothing was missing. Mom and dad never suspected a thing That's how focused I was even then.

The thing that kept driving me was dad's drunkeness. You would never know what would happen to him during a drunk. One time, he ran our only car into a swimming pool. Another time, he traveled from California to Washington during a "drunk blackout;" and didn't even know he had made that long trip, how he'd even gotten to Washington. One time he was so beligerant to another adult that the man broke dad's jaw. He had to eat and drink through a wired jaw for months.

That actually taught him a lesson, I think, because he wasn't so mean to his kids after that. But, by that time, he had already divorced my mother and moved far away . . . to Iceland of all places. There he started another family.

You probably wonder what I did for money to go on a trip to California, right? For weeks and weeks when I wasn't in school, I cut little, short fireplace logs from the local forest and sold these logs for a quarter each to neighbors. I made about twenty dollars, which in 1959 was a lot of money for a kid. I figured I was set.

One Saturday morning in early June, I took off on my adventure. Disneyland here I come.

The weather was nice and I did have on a coat. I hadn't packed any clothes. What I was wearing, I thought, should last me the entire trip. An older friend said a bicycle trip to Anaheim, California, should take about a week. Not knowing any different, I believed him. If I had been a little better at math, I would have calculated that an 1100 plus mile trip like that would have taken eleven-plus days at 100 miles a day, doable for a motivated teenager.

The television weather channel said the weather was going to be nice for a week or so. I had packed enough food in a backpack that it should last about a week, if I didn't eat too much any given day. I wasn't worried at all about water, which there should be plenty of all the way to California.

My map and the ten miles an hour I should be able to make suggested that I could possibly make the Washingon-Oregon border by midnight.

I was off in high spirits, only half a thought of what I would put my mother through. I didn't care what my father thought at all.

My first mistake was not knowing how to adequately read a map. Somehow, I got it turned around. Instead of heading south, as I had planned, I traveled north. By nightfall, following unfamiliar backroads that didn't even seem to be on the map, I got to Everett, Washington, about twenty miles north. That amazed me. How had everything gone so wrong? It had taken me six hours to go twenty miles. At that rate, I would never get to California. And besides, I would need to travel south the same twenty miles just to get past where I lived, south of Mountlake Terrace.

As one of the corollaries to Murphy's Law states: "Everything is more complicated than you think." In my case, even his major law applied: "If anything can go wrong, it will."

As I rode south, reality began to set in. It was already dark, I hadn't brought a sleeping bag, and I was already getting tired. It was obvious now that the trip was way more than I had bargained for. I couldn't use the freeway like cars; I would need to remain on back roads that wound around and around and had lots of stop lights. It would take me weeks, not a week to get to Disneyland.

Not only that, but I would probably look terrible when I got there. Who would hire me then?

It had never occurred to me that Walt Disney would not hire a twelve-year-old without a parent's permission. So, I headed home. It took me until three o'clock in the morning. I knocked on the door. Dad and mom were still up, worrying about me. When I entered the front room, mom threw her arms around me. Dad just gave me a sour look and headed off to bed. Mom wanted to know every little detail, which I gave her. We were both exhausted when we went to our own rooms. My brothers were already sleeping soundly.

What I didn't know was that there were even worse times to come.

# Grizzly Bear Attack

Unbeknownst to me, one of my father's friends thought he had the makings of a naval officer and Kansas was where one needed to attend the Officer Training School. We gave up the house near Lake Ballinger and off we went.

On our way to Kansas, we stopped at Yellowstone National Park in Montana. It was an unusual place where small grizzly bears (not at all as friendly as Yogi and his sidekick) sometimes interacted with humans. I watched one bear enter through the window of a small car. Inside, he began tearing up the upholstery, looking for something he had probably smelled from outside.

The sight was pretty funny looking from far away, but I'll bet the car's owner wasn't pleased when he returned to see the mess the bear had made, getting out of the car.

In those days, there were other animals that would come up to your car . . . animals like big, brown, shaggy buffalos and Roosevelt elk. But even when they did come close, they didn't worry me. Even the bears didn't worry me until one night when I needed to go to the bathroom before going to bed.

The cabin we stayed in didn't have a bathroom; neither did the other cabins. As I remember, there was one or two central out-houses that everyone shared. It wasn't much of a walk to get to one, either.

My mother and I took that walk. About half-way there, a pair of big eyes shined in the darkness. They were high enough above the ground that we knew they were a grizzly bear's eyes. We hurried faster toward the outhouse.

Out of the darkness came the eyes, followed by the bear. What do you do when a big carnivore targets you for dinner? Some people say that since you can't outrun it, you lay down in a foetal position and pretend, like an opossum, that you're dead.

I guess that didn't occur to my mother. Instead, we ran toward the outhouse for all we were worth. We made it just before the grizzly did and mom slammed the door shut and locked it. We could hear the bear wandering around. We could hear low moaning sounds, too. They sounded like bear talk.

Mom was pretty relieved when they stopped. We huddled together in the darkness, afraid to switch the light on. Maybe the bear would think we had magically disappeared and he would go away.

No such luck. Then the outhouse began to shake. Mom screamed. She was pretty sure the bear was going to somehow break through the walls and eat us. I was hoping that whoever had constructed the outhouse had built it strong enough to survive a bear attack.

Mom screamed again. This time it was followed by a, "Help us!"

In a few minutes there was something outside that sounded like a gunshot. I was intrigued. Had someone killed the grizzly?

The cabin shook just a little bit longer and then there was a big "thud". We heard a ranger's voice outside.

It was comforting. "We'll have you out in a few minutes. As soon as we drag the bear away," said the voice.

They did kill it, I thought. Better him than us.

Mom and I heard other male voices. About ten munutes passed before a nice ranger's voice said, "You can come out now. It's safe."

Mom opened the door and looked out cautiously. Three men in uniforms guided my mom and me past a big, hairy lump laying near the door. Even as a pile in the dark, lit only by the nearby cabin lights and the lantern the ranger was holding, it was the largest grizzly I had ever seen.

"How can I thank you?" said my mother. "I don't know what we would have done if you hadn't come."

"There's no thanks needed," said the ranger. "This is why we're here. To protect you from the wildlife. It's their home, too."

Up until then, I had never really thought of it that way. Bears of all kinds are both nocturnal and diurnal. Whenever they're hungry, they're awake. It's always best not to bother them or get in their way. Grizzlies are the biggest apex land predators. They fear nothing. Especially puny looking people.

I was very glad that night to be with my mother and even more happy that a park ranger had tranquilized that big bear. They would take him to the outer edge of the park, where he might stake out another 500 square mile territory far from the cabins. At any rate, I'd be safe in Kansas, far away from him.

# Low Self Esteem

There are times in a person's life when nothing seems to work. That time for me was Olathe, Kansas. I was thirteen and in seventh grade. About the only thing I liked about the school was the history teacher. She was funny.

One day she was talking about Kansas being so hot in the summertime that all the popcorn the farmers' planted had popped in the field. Of course, no-one in class, except me, believed it.

The one thing I did believe was that Kansas had more cockroaches than any other place I had ever seen. They were into everything. In the morning, thousands of them would climb the white fence outside our two-story apartment. Before school, my brother, Stephen, and I made it our duty to kill as many of them as possible with whatever tool was handy—brooms, hammers . . . But every day, more and more would show themselves. It was a losing battle and we humans were losing.

As a younger person, I once tried out to be a Roman Catholic alter boy. I had heard the phrase, "The meek shall inherit the Earth." Seeing all those cockroaches day after day, I was beginning to understand the meaning of that proverb.

Not only were the cockroaches as quick as a mouse, mine could fly. Catching even one of them in the house was a full-time occupation, although it gave me something to do besides school homework.

Kansas was a stressful time in other ways. Money was tight. It had always been on my father's scant military pay, which is why he wanted to become an officer. A child, as I was, certainly doesn't appreciate what it takes to feed a growing family. I just knew that Kansas wasn't the place for me. I resented being there instead of near the ocean, the place I always loved.

I developed the worst case of pimples anyone has ever seen. Kids at school teased me about it. I didn't know (and wouldn't know until I was an adult) that I had an allergy to the stabilizers in chocolate. And a chocolate bar of any kind is what I craved then. I was definitely a chocoholic.

As kids bullied and teased me, I withdrew into myself. I didn't even want to go to school, the only thing I loved about Kansas.

The saving grace for me one day came in the form of a hole, but that hole nearly killed me.

The landlord of our rented house needed a septic tank to be installed. The septic tank needed a hole. I was approached to dig it. Needing the money to buy more chocolate bars, I agreed to dig it for the landlord. For a hole something like ten feet by ten feet by ten feet deep, he would pay me fifteen dollars.

To me, that seemed like a good deal. I was strong and healthy, and I needed something to keep my mind off of cockroaches and pimples. I went to work.

As I recall, it took me two months to dig that hole. After the first month, it was deep enough that I could no longer throw the dirt out of it with a shovel. I had to fill a bucket with a short rope attached and climb out of the hole and empty the bucket by hand away from the hole. That got to be tedious. Finally, my hole was so deep that I had to climb in and out of it using a ladder.

It rained. I was still working inside the deepening hole. It had rained other days, but the rain hadn't bothered me. I heard a strange sound and before I knew it, one wall of the hole collapsed around me. I was stuck up to my waist in dirt and muck.

As the rain came down heavier, dirt started turning into mud. Mud was coming off the walls and seemed to be trying to bury me. I called for help, but no-one came. At least my hands were free and I kept pushing mud away from me as I tried to reach the ladder so I could maybe pull myself up. The mud was getting soupier as more rain and more mud from the walls came down and settled around me.

At last, I heard a car pull into the driveway. I yelled for help. My father came. For the first time in a long time, I was glad to see him.

He found another rope and told me to tie it around my waist, which I did. Then, he began hauling me out, slowly but surely. It was a good thing he did, too, because as he was pulling me up the side of the collapsed bank, it gave way entirely. Had dad not come, I would have been smothered completely. No-one but the entire Olathe Fire Department could have found me. And it probably would have been too late to do me any good.

What happened to the hole? The landlord hired a backhoe to take out all the mud, which is probably what he should have done in the first place, instead of endangering my life. But he did pay me my fifteen dollars.

# Escaping an Elk

Have you ever done something really stupid as a kid, but got away with little or no consequences? I can say through experience that it doesn't happen often.

My fourteenth year on this planet wasn't especially memorable except for two situations that could easily have cost me my short life. In the first situation, two friends and I were visiting the Woodland Park Zoo in Seattle, Washington.

It was a rare, beautiful sunny day in July, one of the Northwest's finest and the three of us were on summer vacation from Junior High School. As you already know, animals have always intrigued me, and except for my grizzly bear encounters when I was younger, no animal has ever frightened me.

When I was feeding five huge hogs in a tight enclosure on my old grandfather's Puyallup, Washington, farm and they pushed me up against a wall, it could have scared me, but then I didn't know that pigs eat people.

In fact, pigs will eat anything. They are consumate omnivores, one reason they are so successful wherever they still live in the wild. But in that pen situation, my stubborn will played out and I fervently pushed back and yelled at the top of my lungs to those pigs, hit one on of them on the top of the head with my slosh bucket, and they all backed off.

So: it was still a bright sunny day when the three of us came to the Roosevelt elk enclosure at the Woodland Park Zoo. When I leaned over to see if there was an elk below the fence separating me from the enclosure, my brand new black plastic comb fell out of my breast pocket and landed in the elk enclosure. I had just bought that comb for ten cents and used it only once.

I looked around the enclosure and the elk were all at the far end of it, laying down, snoozing in the sun. I wasn't thinking exactly right when I climbed the fence and jumped into the elk enclosure to retrieve my comb. The looks on my two friends' faces were incredulous and, of course, I didn't tell them I was going to do it or they would have held me back and told me I was stupid.

At any rate, I bent over, retrieved the comb, and put it in my pants pocket for safe keeping. When I stood upright, in front of me stood the biggest bull elk I had ever seen. We were eyeball to eyeball. I have no idea where he came from.

Now you've heard what happens to stupid people who jump into zoo enclosures with dangerous animals . . . a man was severely mauled by a grizzly bear on one occasion; another man was nearly eaten alive by a Bengal tiger; and another man was pulled right into a chimpanzee enclosure by two strong chimps, which pulled the man under a fence and practically bit off his face. One of the no-nos with chimps is that you don't look them directly in the face–it is a sign of aggression. Sometimes they react violently.

At that moment, looking into the elk's dark brown eyes, I was expecting the worse. Bull elks, like bull moose, will stand on railroad tracks and challenge an oncoming train, so I didn't expect him to get out of my way. And all I could think of, really, was getting back over the fence, back to my friends.

The elk was taller than me and his antlers were easily half my height. Wordless, except for "Hmmm," I asked myself. "What now?" That's when I started feeling seconds as if they were minutes.

I looked up at my two buddies, who were hands against the metal link fence looking down at me. I saw one of them run off, presumably to get a park official to help me.

My situation was starting to look desperate when the big bull elk lowered his antlers, looking like he might scoop me up off the ground and toss me like a sheet of paper into the sky.

What was I to do?

I grabbed hold of his antlers and swung both of my feet to the top of his head between his antlers. He probably felt me standing on his head when he lifted it, and me, effortlessly off the ground. His head kept rising higher and higher.

Soon I could reach the top of the fence and he seemed to be positioning me nearer it. With my hands on the fence and my feet on his head, I somehow climbed up to the top of his antlers. I then scrambled over the top of the fence and was soon standing by both my friends and the park manager, who had all witnessed my precarious escape.

"You know, you could have been killed in there," said the man. "Bull elks are highly territorial." He tried to keep a straight face, but a smile crept out instead.

In those days, I didn't know what territorial meant.

I replied, "Well, I promise I won't go in there again."

My friends and I walked away to yet another exhibit. They didn't say a word to me. When I glanced back at the park person, he had his hands on his hips and was shaking his head.

# Hypothermia

When you're young, there are a lot of big words out there and you don't generally catch their meaning... not until you experience them.

The same mid-July as my awkward elk experience, the same two friends and I were out camping in the woodsy wilderness of the Snowqualmie Forest, not too far from the Greater Puget Sound area.

Now, the real difference between hiking in western and eastern Washington State is that, at that time, there were very few established trails in western Washington. There were, and still are, established trails all over eastern Washington and they connect everywhere. In this kind of situation it is difficult to get lost. Unless... (See the Dead Man's Canyon story.)

When one wants to go hiking in western Washington, it is advisable to take a compass and plot a course to where you intend to go to and where you intend to return to, otherwise, it is easy to get lost. Just ask the Boy Scouts and they will tell you the same thing.

When we started our camping trip, the weather was excellent and in the mountains a bit cooler than at the zoo. We boys thought we had died and gone to heaven as we hiked from the car that had dropped us off to our yet unknown destination. We just thought we would keep hiking and fish along the river.

Our fishing motto was: if you don't get at least a nibble in three casts of your line, move on. Little by little throughout the morning we kept moving up the river. We ended up at a nice glacial lake the river ran out of. Different streams fed into the lake keeping it filled. Near the lake was a wonderful thirty-foot-tall basalt wall that looked climbable; its invitation was too strong to ignore.

One of my buddies and I relieved ourselves of our packs and we started climbing the wall. The smartest one of our trio stayed on the ground, watching us as we climbed higher and higher . . . no petons, or carbiners, no climbing equipment whatsoever.

Within fifteen minutes, both of us were sitting on top of that basalt wall, looking at the lake and our buddy on the ground, who looked a good deal smaller. We both had anticipated going down the other side of the wall, but what we found was a sheer drop-off of at least 100 feet.

If we had tried to de-climb the wall on that side, and fell, we would have landed on rugged sharp-faced basalt that had, over the years, sloughed off from the wall itself. If we had fallen, we certainly would have died there. It appeared our only choice was to decend the wall on the face we had climbed up.

Climbing up is vastly easier than climbing down, especially when you can't see your footholds; it is easy to slip and get yourself into real trouble. Our only other choice was to have the guy on the ground go for help and that didn't seem practical. There were no cell phones in those days and besides, our ride wasn't going to pick us up until the following day and it might have taken our lone companion that long for him to find any kind of help that could rescue us.

"What do you think?" I asked my buddy wall- climber. "If we fall, we are going to badly break something."

"I don't see much of a choice. I don't want to stay up here all night," he said with a groan. He began backing his way down.

"We'd better be real careful," I said, starting down from my location, about two yards away. Foothold after cautious foothold, handhold after cautious handhold we descended. We would stop and look at each other when we were tired. Our arms were getting heavier and heavier, our feet and legs were getting weaker and weaker.

It took nearly an hour to climb down and within ten feet of the ground, we both jumped down. Terra firma never felt so good as when we hit soft soil. We lay there together side by side and our friend just stood staring at us, hands on his hips in kind of a motherly way.

"Okay, okay, you were the smart one," I said.

"I admit it. But the view was great."

And that wasn't even the worst of what was yet to come.

After we revived, we had a lunch of canned pork and beans. I tell you, they tasted like pot roast and all the trimmings.

Both my friend and I were feeling sweaty after the climb, so all three of us went down to the lake.

It was beautiful. All the way around the lake there were fir trees and some Tamaracks. The sun was shimmering off the nearly smooth surface of the lake, looking like someone had strewn diamonds across it. Trout were jumping at flying insects, splashing here and there when they re-entered the lake.

All three of us decided on skinny dipping, since none of us had brought a swim suit. A natural swim, something you can't do in a city pool, would do all of us some good. We stripped down to our birthday suits and decided to swim across the lake to the other side, a distance of perhaps a couple of football fields. About halfway across was a floating fir tree that had fallen into the lake many years previous. It didn't seem to have but a few branch stubs.

"Let's at least swim to the tree and see how we feel," I suggested.

The others agreed and we dove in. After a couple of years of lake swimming after the catfish taught me how to swim, I was feeling pretty confident about my abilities. What I didn't count on was that alpine lakes are a lot colder than Lake Ballinger, where I had first learned to swim.

About ten minutes into the exercise, I started feeling cold penetrate my body. The others were complaining about the same thing. None of us knew anything about hypothermia. I was too young when I lived in Alaska to really understand anything about how the drop in your core body temperature can lead to fatal consequences.

By the time we got to the log. we all realized we might be in some serious trouble. We were having a hard time controlling our legs.

"I'm freezing. Lets hold onto these branch stubs and swim the log back to shore," I suggested.

The others agreed that it was a good idea. "I have a feeling none of us had better let go of this log or we might drown."

With what power we had left, all three of us started swimming that log shoreward.

"I can barely move my legs," said one of my friends.

"Do what you can," the other friend said. "I'm not feeling too bad yet."

Again, seconds felt like minutes as we approached closer and closer to shore. Once we got the log moving, it kept moving. "Keep moving this beast or we will never get to shore," I shouted, colder than ever. "We can't quit."

The seconds were agonizing and pain shot through my legs. I had never felt that before.

"I feel like going to sleep," said the one buddy who was most in distress.

"Slap him if he does," I said to my friend swimming nearer him. "Something tells me he's got to keep awake or its the end for him."

I have no idea how I knew that, but I found out that it was a true statement.

"We're only a thirty yards away from shore. Keep moving. It's taking all of us to move this log. Keep moving, boys, and we'll get there."

The struggle to keep holding onto that log was terrible as pain shot through every single corpuscle in my arms. Moving my legs was getting extremely difficult. I can only imagine what my buddies were going through. Closer to shore . . . closer . . .

Finally, we made it to the sandy bank and all three of us laid there resting in the sunlight, letting the solar warmth heat up our bodies. Nothing ever felt so good. All of us were completely energy drained. We didn't even have enough energy to put on our clothing yet.

I think it was there and then that I realized that my body was an energy receptor, an idea that was to form the basis of my theory and model of behavior, the model I now use.

After a bit more time, we made a campfire. Evening was settling upon us and we cooked most of what was left of our food.

As night fell, we snuggled into our sleeping bags and fell fast asleep. We were so deeply asleep, in fact, that none of us smelled burning leather.

I awoke to a strange smell. I found that the campfire had creeped to one of my hiking boots and during the night, it had been roasted. I put on my good shoe and I tied plastic bags that had once contained some of the food we had each brought around my other foot.

The hike out of the forest to the car that was awaiting us was the longest, most slippery hike I had ever made.

But, at least none of us suffered frost-bitten fingers or frost-bitten legs, often a result of severe hypothermia. I thank the sun for that.

What did I learn from those two strange experiences? Nature has spectacular surprises for those who challenge her. Beware!

# Gymnastics

All during high school, the sport I liked best was gymnastics. By and large, it is an individual sport. You do the best you can through continual practice and after extensive training, you don't have to depend upon a crowd to continue your work.

People good at gymnastics generally have great bodies, have great poise when they are walking, and also have terrific personalities. On top of that, they are both mentally and physically fit and aren't as "stuck up" as football players or basketball players.

Over my three years of high school, I got better at gymnastics than I did at anything else. I was okay at all the individual parts of the sport—the high bar, the parallel bars, the floor exercise, the rings—but my speciality became the Arabian handspring; it is a most unusual maneuver.

There are three basic parts to an Arabian handspring. First, there is the run. The run gives one the momentum to accomplish the second part—a simultaneous horizontal head-long jump with a high arch. The third and most critical part is the head-tucked-in rolling landing. If all three parts aren't done well, the stunt doesn't look right. If the rolling landing isn't accomplished well, you can end up languishing in a hospital somewhere with a broken neck or back.

It took me two full years to create the most beautiful spectacle, the most exciting Arabian handspring anyone had ever seen. Despite its difficulty, I never once did it wrong enough to hurt myself, because if a person lands wrong, he could actually break his neck or ruin his spinal cord. Each time I performed an Arabian during a school assembly or during the half-time of a football or basketball game, the audience would "Oooh" and "Awww" appreciatively.

What I wasn't so good at—the high bar—is what nearly killed me. That didn't come until I was in my first year and a half at the University of Washington.

What I really wanted, in addition to doing an excellent Arabian was to be a great all-around gymnast, the kind you see at the Olympics. In order to do that one has to master all the different aspects that I related to before. My worst performances were on the high bar and I was dedicated to improving them. I spent hours before my classes began and hours after my classes ended trying to get my high bar routine better and better.

One day, I guess I was more tired than normal. I put the white chalk on my hands and rubbed it around the crevices. I jumped up on the horizontal bar a couple of feet above my head and started my swing. No problem so far.

I felt ready to do a series of "eagles"—full body rotations around the bar at some speed. I was just learning how good they felt when one's hands, wrists, arms, torso and legs were all working together to emit that perfect series of rotations.

Then it happened. During the second rotation, one of my hands slipped off the bar and the other hand followed. Precariously, my momentum kicked in and I was thrown about ten feet away from the equipment. The bad news was that I had dislocated my left shoulder. The good news is that I had not landed on my head or neck, which could have killed me instantly. It has happened to other novice gymnasts.

I blacked out completely.

The next thing I remember was the awful scent of smelling salts under my nose. They awoke me.

The gymnastics instructor said, "Robert, you have a dislocated shoulder and maybe a fractured collar bone. This is going to hurt like hell, but I've got to put your shoulder back in its socket before all the muscles contract. If I don't do this now, it will be much, much harder later. The other guys are going to hold you down."

He didn't give me an opportunity to object.

I felt an awful wrenching on my shoulder and then yelled through the terrific pain I was experiencing. The pain went away suddenly.

After that, all I felt was a dull aching.

"Better now?" he asked.

I nodded.

"Now the boys and I are going to gently lift you off the floor and take you to the University nurse. She'll do the rest."

Of course, I didn't know what "the rest" meant, but I was eager enough to get off the floor where gravity was sinking my shoulder into the floor.

I was incredibly thankful that I had so good and knowledgable a gymnastics teacher that he was able to put me back together.

For close to three months, an entire quarter of school, I wore a sling to school every day. The worst part wasn't the sling. The worst part is that I was left-handed. These were the days before computers and I couldn't afford a typewriter. I had homework to do, term papers to write. I had to learn all over again how to write, right-handed this time. My teachers at first complained of how sloppy was my printing, although I was trying my best. Finally with practice, it, too, improved. Today, as a result, I am ambidexrous.

Sports are opportunities for just about anything to happen. Even when the practice effect and muscle memory take effect, there are rigorous exercises involved. Team sports, in my opinion, are even more likely to cause an accident resulting in an injury, simply because there are more people involved, and more of a chance for chaos to rein.

Given all this, however, the best prepared person is still the most practiced person. In sports, as in most other endeavors, there is no substitute for just good old plain hard work.

# The Tower

L ife is full of decisions and full of ifs. One seldom knows what choice to make, but if you make the right choice at about the right time, you usually fair pretty well.

I come from a military family on my father's side and a farming family on my mother's side. Since I was very young, I have been empathetic to everyone and everything (although I admit I once got so mad at a younger brother that I nearly threw him out a second story window.)

Being empathetic probably comes from the farming side of the family, since having patience and protecting things are essential qualities to being a good gardener and farmer; they plant things and watch them grow.

My military side is more like creating chaos and destroying things.

I am pleased my farming side usually wins over, because I believe that if something is born and matures, it has a right to continue to exist. That includes wildlife and most plants.

During the Vietnam War, I was exactly what the military was seeking. I was young, smart, exceptionally physically fit, and in my last year of high school—a prime target for induction.

Since my empathetic side overrules my aggressive side, I decided I didn't want to kill anyone in a war, at least not if I could help it. I didn't want to put myself into a situation in which it was either "him or me," the exact situation you so often find in war.

I've also seen what happens to soldiers. When someone kills another person, he often has big regrets during the rest of his life. It's not an accident that many military men commit suicide. Sometimes the regret is so deep and painful, it hurts. In order to keep some sort of sanity in his life, the military person concocts some rationalization that keeps him sane. Or, others create that rationalization for him.

At any rate, the US Army was out of the question for me. The Air Force was appealing, but I don't normally get excited about being in high places. My father was a Navy man, but riding on top of big waves makes me somewhat seasick and there are plenty of those in the ocean.

What was left? The Submarine Service seemed to be my answer. At least, I would be under the big waves, not riding on top of them.

The whole idea of run silent, run deep and the silent service was intriguing. I had seen the television episodes of submarine warfare and though I didn't like the torpedo-killing-people- part, I wouldn't have to look eyeball to eyeball at another person who might be killed. And what better place to not kill anyone in a shore war than in a submarine.

It didn't occur to me that living in a World War II kind of diesel submarine might actually be dangerous.

My submarine training started at the Armory in Seattle, Washington, where we actually had our own real-life submarine. As a reserve in the Navy, I practiced on it every other weekend while I was also attending the University of Washington. Being aboard that sub was truly great training for what was to come a year later when I ran out of college money and went on active duty.

"Qualifying" to become a submariner requires a great memory. One must learn the on and off positions of every valve on a submarine, when it should be open and when it should be closed. Additionally, one needs sharp eyes, because one of your duties might be as a lookout, one of two that stands with the captain or executive officer on the bridge of the boat when it is on the surface.

The reason I bring this up is that one night on patrol in the South China Sea, I was one of those two lookouts. Ships and boats, like us, didn't use running lights at night. This was particularly hazardous, but it was also war-time.

In the darkness on a moonless night, all a lookout can see is someone with a cigarette in his mouth (up to ten miles away) or the silhouette of a ship that passes close by. That's it.

As I was looking through my binoculars, I saw the looming silhouette of a Russian destroyer. By the time I could actually tell what it was, that ship was ready to ram our submarine. It wasn't intentional, his lookouts simply didn't see us. Since the ship was approaching from my side of our sub, our other lookout didn't see it, either.

I screamed at the young captain, "Captain, destroyer coming right at us!"

The captain whirled around and saw the huge shadow approaching at great speed. He yelled down through the open hatch to the helmsman in the tall metal sail, "ALL BACK EMERGENCY!"

The helmsmen was awake, thank God, and did as he was hold. Our boat promptly backed up in emergency mode and we just barely missed being crushed to death by that shadowy destroyer. Whew! Close call!

At this point, I've actually gotten ahead of my story, so let's back up. Before I survived this near catastrophe, I had to survive a near-death experience in a tall cylinder called, "The Tower."

There are quite a few things in life that are counter-intuitive; that is, on the surface, they don't sound logical.

"Eat your vegetables," is one of these. To a kid, a lot of vegetables don't taste good. But when one grows older and learns about nutrician and what the body needs in the way of vitamins and minerals, the advice makes sense.

If you were underwater, swimming for all you were worth to get to the surface and someone told you to keep exhaling your breath, that would seem counter-intuitive. Right? The advice would sound strange. What if I do get to the surface and I can't inhale because there is no breath left in me to exhale so I can take another breath. Now, that's quite a conundrum for a teenager that only learned to swim about seven years before, taught by a catfish.

Let me explain.

When you breathe above water and you dive, the air in your lungs compresses, as does the rest of your body. However, when you breathe underwater, as from an aqualung or in a submarine, depending upon how deep you are, the breath in your lungs exponentially expands precipitously the closer you get to the surface.

Inside the submarine, there is a controlled atmosphere so your lungs accommodate, but if you breathe inside and go outside into the surrounding ocean, your body must re-accommodate to the outside pressure.

Why was this so important to me?

This was the background necessary to save my life when I entered the tower, a huge 100-foot-tall cyclinder, maybe twenty feet wide at Pearl Harbor, Hawaii.

Inside the cylinder, filled with water, is where submariners learn how to save their own lives when a submarine is drowned.

During WWII, it was found that if a submarine had an accident or was depth-charged or torpedoed, but could hover and maintain a depth of somewhere around 300 feet deep, the sailors inside that sub might be able to save their own lives. The sub captain might be lucky enough even to find the ocean shallow enough so he could sit the submarine on the bottom at about 300 feet deep.

In any case, all but one of the submariners could possibly escape through the torpedo tubes. In order to do this, one man had to stay behind and operate the torpedo tubes so his crewmates could escape. That man would die alone.

The tower was designed to train escaping submariners how NOT to hold their breathe when they exited a torpedo tube and headed for the surface.

In the morning of a particularly nice October Hawaiian day, I found myself in a bathing suit in the airlock of "The Tower." My instructor gave me the last rites.

"From here, you will swim up the 100 feet to the top of the water column. Do Not hold your breath. Say, "Ha . . . ha . . . ha . . . all the way up."

"You're joking right? You don't really want me to talk underwater."

"That's exactly what I want you do," he said. "When you're saying ha . . . ha . . . ha . . . you will be releasing the air that will be expanding in your lungs while you are heading to the surface. If you don't release that air, when you get to the surface, your lungs will explode and YOU WILL DIE."

At that point in my life, I had never read a scuba book. I didn't know that what he was telling me was absolutely true.

The watertight door, leading to the water column was to my left, the other watertight door, leading to the safety of the outdoors from where I had come from, was on my right. I was seriously debating which door to go through.

To me, just trying to swim up through 100 feet of water to reach the surface seemed like an impossible task, especially since I was only going to be able to take a single breath of air to do it. No extra air, no scuba tanks, nothing . . . just me and my two lungs.

After a few minutes of silent debate with myself, the instructor prompted me with, "If you do not pass this test, you will not be able to become a submariner."

"If I don't pass this test, I'll probably be dead anyway," I replied.

He laughed. "Don't worry so much. There are observers stationed in scuba about every thirty feet. If they don't see you exhaling, one or more of them will sock you in the stomach and make you exhale."

I grimaced. "Then I'll have a really sore stomach."

"It's better than dying," he said as he smiled. "You'll make it. I have faith in you."

He hit the valve to bring water into the water-tight chamber and the water level rose around us.

As soon as the water was up to my neck, he said, "Okay, breathe normally and I'll send you out."

"You're not going with me?"

"No, I remain in here and get ready for the next fellow."

Now I knew I was alone. I didn't want to look like a coward. Whatever happened, whatever I could do to stay alive is what I would do. I had to have faith in my instructor and hoped to heaven he knew what he was doing.

The added pressure when I entered the water column was truly amazing. My ears tried to pop and I was able to equalize the pressure in them. It was a good thing I didn't have a cold or that might have been impossible.

The water wasn't as cold as the ocean would be, athough there there was a lot of it, and because I wasn't wearing a mask, the view was terribly hazy.

I started kicking for all I was worth. As I passed markers on the inside of the water column, I could feel my lungs filling up with more air. The air was making me buoyant and helping me rise toward the surface. I started my ha . . . ha . . . ha . . . Amazingly, I kept rising.

I saw the hazy figure of a man in scuba as I passed a few feet from him at a depth of 60 feet. I kept rising, still talking underwater.

I saw another hazy figure at about 30 feet.

"Ha . . . ha . . . ha . . ."

I could see light at the surface. I kicked even harder. "Ha . . . ha . . . ha . . ."

No-one had ever been more pleased with himself when he broke the surface than I was then. What an experience!

# Manana Island and Turtle Island

There are two places not mentioned in Hawaiian travel guides—Manana Island (commonly known to locals as Rabbit Island) and Turtle Island. Both small islands lie just north, about a mile, off of Makapuu Point on the island of Oahu in the Hawaiian Island Chain. Makapuu Point is the home of the incredibly wonderful oceanarium, Sea Life Park, and its research affiliate, The Oceanic Institute, both places at which I have studied.

The reason you will not find Rabbit Island and Turtle Island mentioned in the Hawaiian travel guides is that both places are very, very dangerous. I contracted lava poisoning on Turtle Island and nearly lost my life near Rabbit Island, and this is what actually happened.

While doing intensive cetacean research at both Sea Life Park and the Oceanic Institute, I often wondered what was on the rabbit-shaped island. I saw flocks of seabirds ringing it and figured it was a nesting area for gulls and possibly other kinds of seabirds. Since I have always had an avid interest in birding and in animal behavior specifically, I thought it might be worth my time to swim to Rabbit Island and get a closer look.

I planned my trip carefully, knowing there would be some sort of north to south current between Makapuu Point and Rabbit Island.

Waimanalo is the only town in the area north of Makapuu point but there are numerous small jump-off points where one can park a small motorcycle and enter the ocean. Since it was to be a summer day trip, I wore only a pair of swim trunks, a mask and snorkel, and swim fins. The weather was gorgeous—warm with a bit of sea breeze. I left about 10:00 AM.

The water was shallow when I entered the ocean channel and kept getting deeper as I swam further into it. The current wasn't as strong as I suspected it would be, but it was carrying me southward and a bit eastward toward Rabbit Island. The water was crystal clear; I could see all the way to the bottom of the channel, a depth of about ten fathoms (sixty feet). The first sea life I spotted was a school of large jacks which barely took notice of me swimming on the surface. Then I saw a spotted eagle ray, a beautiful site, and I dived down about five fathoms to get a better look at it. It saw me coming, turned around, and sped away. I resurfaced for air.

About five minutes later, I spotted a black and white krait coming up to the surface to breathe. A venomous sea snake wasn't at all what I expected to see. I had read they were extremely dangerous with enough venom in them to kill a dozen men. As importantly, kraits are even more dangerous during their summer to fall mating period when they become territorial. I certainly did not want to tangle with a six-foot snake that could swim as fast as I could. I watched it intently as I swam along and it surfaced, breathed, and dove.

I turned even more southward to avoid it, but it kept coming toward me while submerged. Before I knew it, that aggressive krait had bitten my right flipper and all I could do was to try to dislodge it with my left flipper. If it had bitten me on an exposed ankle, I wouldn't be writing this. After a few seconds that seemed like minutes, the krait loosened its grip and turned around. I guess it figured I had gotten the message to stay out of its vertical territory.

At that moment, I should have turned westward and headed for Makapuu point, not far away, but I didn't. It was a bad decision to continue my adventure, because the rest of the trip was to be much worse.

The current quickened and I was carried me past Rabbit Island to Turtle Island, where I had not intended to land at all. Even from Sea Life Park, I could tell it was a desolate lava sea-mount, something that had risen ages before from the sea floor. I was getting tired, however, and the island looked like a convenient stopping point. I suspected that I would be swimming against the current to get to Rabbit Island, about an eighth of a mile to the north and I would need the rest.

The small island was very rugged and jagged lava prevented me from getting on the island with my flippers on. Bare feet were exposed to the lava as I climbed on the island on its western shore. Nothing more than spiders and seabird dung was on Turtle Island and I sat there for half an hour deliberating my next moves while spiders moved all around me. Fortunately, they weren't poisonous spiders and they didn't recognize me as lunch.

I headed to the northern side of small Turtle Island and put my swim fins back on. (Little did I know that I had already contracted a life-threatening bacterial infection.) Then I slipped into the channel between Rabbit Island and Turtle Island. The current was swifter than I had ever imagined and something unexpected happened.

The current swept me right into a toilet bowl kind of area on the southern side of Rabbit Island. As I looked up, I could see the big island rising straight up like the rock of Gibraltar. There was no place to exit the water, no place to get on the island. I would need to swim around back to the western side of the island where it sloped gradually or around the island on its seaward side where I had never been able to see, and knew not what to expect.

The water was still crystal clear below me, but every few minutes it would cloud with bubbles as a new wave entered the bowl. A few large fish were swimming in it amidst boulders the size of small houses. What I was to experience next was beyond imagining.

The next wave was like an ebb-tide and sucked me underwater nearly to the bottom of the bowl. Aboard the submarine while at sea I had practiced holding my breath for up to two and a half minutes, so I was prepared for such submergence. The current tossed me right against one of the big boulders. The water clouded and for a time I couldn't tell which way was up and which way was down.

My ears, however, were stinging so I knew I was at least thirty feet down. I equalized and the stinging stopped. About the time my lungs started aching, a fresh current pushed me back to the surface where I started hyperventilating in earnest.

Another wave came in. Uncontrollably, back down I went, this time against another large boulder. I could already tell my back and arms were being scratched to pieces by the rough-edged boulders. The water clouded with bubbles. Something large and swift came near me. I couldn't make out what it was, but I hoped I wasn't bleeding and it wasn't a lemon shark, a bull shark, or a tiger shark, all of which have nurseries in the shallows of the Hawaiian Islands, and all of which are man eaters.

I was almost out of air again. Another wave came in and its current raised me to the surface where I could breathe. My energy was draining away. How long could I keep this up? Would I eventually drown in this unlikely place? If I did, no-one would certainly ever know where I had gone to. I had only told a few submariner friends that I was swimming to Rabbit Island.

Now I was glad that no-one had decided to come with me, because I could not have rescued them if I had tried. The intermittent waves were so strong, I couldn't even defend myself against them.

Down into the depths I went again. This time my hyperventilation had been insufficient and my lungs were suffering. I could see spots before my eyes, a certain sign of stress.

I could feel myself being bashed against another hard surface and I was underwater for what seemed like a long time. I started kicking for the surface for all I was worth. So far, at least, the current hadn't torn off my tight-fitting swim fins.

When I was within sight of the bubbly surface, the current raised me up the rest of the way and I lay on the surface panting heavily through my snorkel. My mask was filling up with water and I had time enough to drain it before another wave current dragged me back under again.

I do not know how many times I was submerged, nor how many times I was raised to the surface, where each time I desperately needed air, but I finally gave up completely. I no longer had enough energy to even kick my feet. I barely had enough energy to breathe.

While I was submerged, I remember saying to myself, "This is it. This is where I will die. Take what nature is offering. I won't be getting out of this." My lungs were aching; my shoulders and back were stinging. I don't know why, but I tore off my mask and snorkel and they drifted away. I shut my eyes. I didn't have enough energy left to take off my swim fins.

Surfers say that the seventh wave is the strongest. Maybe for me it was, because the next wave that entered the bowl tossed me completely clear of it and I found myself in deeper ocean in a current that was heading down the coast of Oahu. I drifted with the current. Eventually, I found a beach and crawled up, laying there for an hour, recuperating.

When I recovered, I hitch-hiked north to where I had parked my motorcycle. But that is not the end of this story.

A few days later, my body showed sever signs of cellulitis, a bacterial infection, leading to cell breakdown. The bacteria on the lava of Turtle Island had entered tiny cuts in my feet while I had been walking across the lava. The bacteria spread quickly up my legs to my groin and into my lymph nodes.

In a few more days, I could not walk at all. I placed myself in the care of the Navy doctors at Pearl Harbor. For the next three weeks, they pumped me full of tetramyacin and other newer anti-bacterial drugs. Thankfully, the drugs worked and killed the infection. I probably would have died otherwise.

What did I learn from this misadventure? There are reasons some places are not listed in tourist guides; locals know to avoid such places. Sometimes it is best not to invite friends to go on adventures where you do not know what to expect. Also, nature is powerful at her best, devastating to human beings and other animals at her worst. It is impossible to plan for every contingency, but being the best prepared you can be is better than little or no preparation at all.

Yet another thing I learned was that what you tell yourself is sometimes wrong, dead wrong. I am highly intuitive, a facility I have had since I was at least fifteen years old. But nothing told me that I should not swim to Rabbit Island, nor that I would leave that place alive. Intuition, therefore, must be geared to past experiences, because generally my intuition is right on spot, anticipating personal near future events, which has always given me an edge. Intuition has helped me in my business dealings and lately in my favorite gambling games—Texas Hold'em Poker and Baccarat, the James Bond game, invented way back when by Italians. My intuition totally failed me in all cases concerning Manana Island.

# Sudden Death on a Busy Freeway

Life experiences can be valuable when viewed through the lens of, "What would I do differently?" This is a story about stupidity, something I would definitely not do again.

When one is writing an autobiography, one has to be a hundred percent honest not only with the reader, but with himself. A writer cannot gloss over things or change things just to make himself look smarter.

I am writing this story for for a couple more reasons. Firstly, I want to relate how ridiculous a nneteen-year-old male can be even when he is thinking clearly and not even under the spell of drugs or alcohol. If I had been using drugs or alcohol, I would have had an excuse for what you are going to read, but I was clean in all respects. Secondly, I want to impress upon young people just how deadly going the wrong way on a freeway can be.

Nearly everyone in the world by now has probably seen a Hollywood car chase on a freeway, where a vehicle, for one reason or another, is traveling in the wrong direction. In movies, these scenes are highly controlled using special drivers, restricted spaces, and walkie-talkies between the director of the film and his actors. Nothing is left to chance. If something was, there would most likely be a death on the freeway during filming and perhaps the end of making that film. Someone might even spend time in jail.

In most places in the world, there are signs on freeways at tricky places designating "Wrong Way" or "Do Not Enter." These signs are important, worthy of a driver's attention. They are not to be ignored.

On this particular warm spring day in Hawaii, I was on my Honda motorcycle and I had a girl in back of me, her arms around my waist, holding tightly. I didn't tell her what I was about to do. . . stupid thing number one. Of course, because she liked me so much, she would have talked me out of it. Stupid thing number two is that even though I cared for her, too, I was not thinking of her saftety, much less mine.

Riding a freeway in the wrong direction had been on my mind for some time. You see, I was thinking about becoming a Hollywood stunt man after my service was over and after I had gotten my Bachelor of Arts degree. After all, I was a gymnast and really good at falling down. So: I really did want to experience riding on a motorcycle going the wrong way on a freeway.

Strange logic isn't it? Stupid logic isn't it?

Shirley was at her wits end when I turned onto the off-ramp. Suddenly, she knew what was going to happen.

"Let me off! I don't want to die yet!" she screamed over the engine roar.

"No. Just hang on tight. Nobody is dying today!" I yelled back.

We started up the off-ramp. So far so good. There were no cars coming down. Shirley was quiet after that, and probably shutting her eyes tightly.

Mine were wide open and both riders were wearing helmets, not that that would have made any difference if a car had hit us.

Once on the freeway, I had about five seconds to react. I saw the first car coming in our lane (her lane) at the speed limit, which was at least fifty miles and hour. We were going nearly as fast. I pulled over as close to the left hand barrier as I could, which was her right lane. The female driver had no time to use her horn and she missed us an inch. I heard an incredibly loud "Whoosh!" as her car passed by.

The next driver in the same lane, a male this time, did have some time and he leaned on his horn. It was an instant Doppler Effect as I heard his horn in the near distance intensify, come to a sharp peak when he also barely missed us, and then gradually decline in intensity as the car continued down the freeway.

I saw a row of cars coming this time, but they were still in the distance. The experience was enough for me and I made a sharp turn on the freeway within two lanes and headed for the same exit that Shirley and I had come up. By the time I was turned around, the row of cars was just behind us. I zipped the motorcycle into the right lane and soon speeded down the off-ramp. No-one followed.

I was going so fast, however, that Shirley and I ended up in the shallow ditch alongside the off-ramp.

Thank God both of us were all right . . . no bumps, no bruises, even from quick-landing in the ditch. I pledged to Shirley then and there that I would never do anything so stupid again.

That both cars missed us was a miracle given that the drivers had so very little time to react. I learned that day how incredibly fast vehicles approach each other at 100 miles an hour, fifty miles for each vehicle going in the opposite direction.

We never did tell her wonderful parents about the episode, because being sane, they would have insisted that I never see their daughter again. And Shirley and I never did discuss how "interesting" that experience had been for her.

Changing times and different paths took me away from becoming a Hollywood stunt man, although I was to suffer many more falls. Shirley married a high school sweetheart and had four beautiful children, which are now all adults.

Had the day been slightly different by an inch or so, neither she nor I would have had more of a life. It would have been sudden death on a freeway.

# Alcohol Poisoning

There is a long-standing tradition among submariners. When one graduates to being an actual submariner, other bona fide submariners of your crew take you to the nearest bar. But before I get to that episode, let me fill you in on why that tradition exists.

Submarines are complex machines. They not only need to be water-tight, but they also need to rise and sink. Rising and sinking are achieved by leveraging water ballast from one tank to another and by taking on water or releasing it into the sea. To do that, there are a series electrically controlled valves, and other essential equipment. Also, there are bow planes that control the angle of a boat's rise or fall and stern planes which do much the same for the rear end of the vessel. If everything is going right, the captain is a happy person. If everything is going wrong, the entire crew could die.

So, to become a bona fide submariner, there is one hell of a lot to learn and each sub that one rides is somewhat different than the next one. A person has to qualify on each and every submarine. During my career, I traveled on four of them. That means I had to learn every the function of every valve, the placement of every electrical line, how to fight a fire aboard a sub, and a hundred other technical things about each boat. (A submarine is classified as a boat; a destroyer or bigger vessel is referred to as a ship.)

Of course, learning these things aren't easy, either, because all the while you are expected to be doing your job, whatever that is. I was a sonarman which meant I was the eyes and ears of the submarine while it was underwater. In what spare time I had, I learned everything I needed to know from manuals and practical experience. And eventually, I qualified.

The big day of my graduation arrived when I passed my tests, written and practical.

A few of the qualified submariners took me to a bar in Seattle. They showed me the silver dolphins I was about to place on my blue Navy uniform proudly. But instead of handing the insignia to me, they told the bartender to fill up a quart glass pitcher with a little of everything on the back bar. It surprised me, even more, when the bartender brought the full pitcher to my bar stool and when one of the men dropped my silver dolphins into the alcohol solution.

They sank to the bottom of the pitcher.

"Now chug-a-lug and catch the dolphins in your teeth," the Chief of the Boat said.

"You mean I have to drink all that?" I replied.

He nodded, "And catch the dolphins in your teeth."

"Well...okay," I said. I didn't try to explain to the chief that I wasn't a drinker. I could nurse a beer or a rum and coke all night when necessary.

Now, one needs to appreciate what was in that concoction. A little bit of everything in a bar can cause alcohol poisoning big time. Of course, being young and not a drinker, I didn't know that at the time. Various kinds of alcohol have different strengths. Some brands are 50 proof, some are 150 proof. And then there was the fact that no-one told me you were supposed to go to the nearest bathroom after you had drunk the quart of fluid and then vomit it back out.

Preserving the submarine tradition, I drank the entire quart and caught the dolphins in my teeth. Shortly after, I passed out. Apparently, the Chief of the Boat and the others in my crew didn't know much about my non-drinking habits.

I didn't feel the ride back to my house in the car that the commander of the submarine was driving. He arrived with me back to my house.

My mother helped me to bed and I didn't wake up for two days. When I did wake up, I had the dolphins clutched into my left hand.

# Submarine Sounding

Have you ever been so closely tuned into someone else that you know exactly when they died, and as a result, you almost did, too?

If graduation from high school was important to me, graduation from college was even more important. All the men in my family as far back as I can trace their genealogy all died young, very young. Many died in wars, some died in accidents, some probably even died from diseases and the Bubonic Plague that swept Europe during the Dark Ages. But the fact that I am here, and you are here, means that at least the women in our families survived long enough to raise the next generation.

None of my family older than me was ever educated to the degree that I was. No-one older than me ever got that kind of opportunity. I often heard my father say that he never made it past lieutenant in the military, because he didn't have a college degree. How he wished he had my opportunity. So, you see, it was so important to me to make the most of going to a university. And I did. That experience is something I would wish on anyone.

After more than a year at the University of Washington, it was time for me to go on active duty with the Submarine Service. I had spent a previous summer at Hunter's Point in San Francisco, going to Submarine School and training with marines at Submarine Boot Camp. I did pretty well after the first week and graduated both. I was well on my way to becoming a submariner.

(I am not going to name the four submarines that I qualified and worked on. That is still a confidential matter, according to the

Submarine Service, and something I still cannot divulge due to a secrecy agreement I signed.)

So, on with the story . . .

My grandmother, Tomasina Rota, and I had telepathic communication with each other at long distances since I was born. Who knows why? Maybe it was just a freak of nature. At any rate, this is how I confirmed it in her last few minutes.

I was now aboard a World War II vintage submarine operating the twin stern planes. These paddle-like structures at the rear and on each side of the sub control the angle of dive of a submarine and as such they are incredibly important. Another man beside me was operating the twin bow planes, which control the dive itself. Both men work together to control both the rise and dive of a submarine. They need to work in perfect balance together. Of the planes, however, the stern planes are more important to a dive.

The instant my grandmother died, I felt instantly sick to my stomach, as if a severe flu had attacked my body. The overbearing feeling spread throughout my body and within seconds I went completely comitose. It was as if my body had left its physical dimensions to join my grandmother's. Essentially, I now believe, I was experiencing her death with her.

The Chief of the Boat was standing directly behind me when the bubble in front of me started rising dramatically and the submarine went into a steep dive. He must have said to me, "Hult, what's going on? Get your bubble back." However, in my comitose state, I didn't hear him.

The Chief of the Boat supervises both planesmen during a dive. On the captain's orders, he also shifts water from ballast tank to ballast tank to control both the diving and surfacing of the submarine.

Before I blanked out, we had been at 100 feet below the surface. I am told that we were at 200 feet deep when the C.O.B. started shouting at me. I didn't respond.

By the time the submarine had sank at an even steeper angle to 400 feet, everyone was concerned, including the captain in the conning tower above us. He hadn't ordered "test depth," which is where things on older submarines start groaning and causing concern.

When we were at 600 feet deep, the C.O.B. ordered someone else to take my place at the stern planes. When we were at 800 feet deep, the "crush depth" of the submarine, people were trying to get me to release the death grip I had on the stern planes wheel. The bubble was at maximum angle to dive and coffee cups and any number of other things (I am told) were flying around the cabin and all over the submarine within each compartment.

I had been comitose for nearly five full minutes when I finally revived. I found myself in my bunk in the after battery compartment of the submarine. I had no recollection of anything besides being incredibly sick and then a total blank-out . . . not a black out. It was as if my spirit and all the energy I had went somewhere else.

I saw no white light, nothing at all spiritual. I was just gone, gone from my body.

The next day I was in front of the captain in his room. I couldn't explain what had happened. He dismissed me and said he would have to file a report. It would go into my record.

The next day, he called me into his room again. This time, it was to tell me that my Italian grandmother had died. I asked him if he could find out what day and time she had died. He did.

Both he and I were amazed to find out that given the difference between the time zone that she was in and the time zone that we were in, the time she had died was the instant I had become sick and then blanked out. At first, neither the captain nor I could believe it, but it was confirmed.

The captain never wrote that report and it didn't enter my record. There are some things in our world that are still unexplainable to modern science. Telepathy of the kind that I describe here apparently is one of them.

# One Cold January Morning

To pay tuition as a student at the University of Washington in Seattle, I was working in a restaurant as a busboy and dish washer. The pay was minimum wage, but it did help me also pay the monthly rent on a one bedroom downstairs apartment a couple blocks away from Green Lake.

The restaurant was on San Point Way, several miles west of my apartment. The university was about the same distance from the apartment but in a little different direction. I thought I had it made.

My transportation, besides normal bus routes was a Honda CL90cc motorcycle, a classy little job that got about sixty miles to a gallon of gas. Gas in my "good old days" was about forty cents a gallon and it was the age of muscle cars.

Nobody really cared how much gas they burned, but as a student my funds were definitely restricted, which is why the Green Lake area was so good for me. I could run completely around the lake on an established trail and watch the wildlife on the lake at the same time. Ducks and geese, especially, loved the lake as much as I did.

This tragic night, as I recall, was very cold and in the middle of January. The restaurant's owner had taken a liking to me and trusted me to close up his establishment every night. I worked to about 2:30 AM in the morning, a half hour after he closed his bar. I bussed what few tables I hadn't already cleaned and washed all the remaining dishes to get them ready for the next day's customers. The place looked decent.

In those days, I could afford few clothes and I had almost no winter clothes at all. I was, however, a scuba diver, and I had a full wet suit. I put it over my work clothes, put on my motorcycle helmet, and locked the door to the restaurant. I was off, riding the motorcycle along the deserted streets of San Point Way. I turned right onto another vacant city street and headed west toward my apartment.

The rest of the night was to be a nightmare!

A little more than halfway home, I was nearly through an intersection on my green light when out of nowhere, a sedan ran a red light and hit me broadside. The car impacted me so severely that my left leg contacted the shift handle, went through my leg, and broke the handle completely off the bike. I shot into the air as if I had been shot from a circus cannon. As I sailed away from the bike almost twenty feet in the air, I kept going a distance of nearly fifty feet.

Just before I made contact with the ground, I tucked into a roll and when I did hit the pavement of the street, I bounced like a big rubber ball. I kept rolling another ten feet or so before I stopped.

I lay there for the longest time, feeling for broken bones. If it hadn't been for my gymnastic training in high school and college, I surely would have been dead right there on the spot. If I hadn't been wearing my helmet, I would have been dead; if I hadn't rolled to dissipate the energy of the crash, I would have been dead. But my problems were not yet over.

The young driver of the sedan, much to his credit, did not run away. Rather, he stayed and asked me if I was okay. I said yes. Another passerby saw the mangled motorcycle and called the police. When they arrived, the sedan driver told the truth—it had been his fault. He had run a red light and had hit me squarely broadside, knocking me the distance of sixty feet away from my transportation, where I still lay, a bit stunned, but okay, or so I thought.

I felt a little numbness in my left leg, but otherwise I felt fine and the officer had me get to my feet. He quizzed me and I had all the right answers. He asked if I wanted him to take me to hospital. I declined. Instead, I asked him to take me to my apartment. I thought I only needed some sleep.

He continued to do his police duty and took statements from me and the sedan driver. The young man had just gotten word that his girlfriend was pregnant and was serving him a court paternity suit. I never heard from or contacted that young man again, but I still thank him for his complete honesty; it served him well, because I would never sue someone that forthright.

When the officer took me home, he saw that I was bleeding a bit from my left leg and he asked me a few more questions. "Are you sure you don't want to go to the hospital and let them check you over?"

"No thanks, I feel okay," I said and unlocked the door to my apartment. I waved goodbye and that fine gentleman left.

About fifteen minutes later, I started feeling peculiar. It was the beginning of the ordeal. I had never been in shock before; I didn't know the symptoms.

I started shivering, then shaking so badly that all I wanted was some heat on my body. I turned the oven up to 500 degrees, opened the oven door, and pulled up a chair. Even after five minutes, I couldn't feel the heat. I went into the bathroom and turned the hot water faucet on full. I put myself into a tub of near scalding water. I couldn't feel the heat even though my body was turning a brilliant red. My mind simply wasn't functioning properly.

Fortunately, I did have a telephone and more fortunately than that my best friend's mother was a registered nurse. I called her. From my quavering voice and the best description I could give her, she realized I was in terrifically bad shape. At about 4AM, she came over to my apartment, called one of the clinic doctors where she worked, and got him out of bed. We all met at the clinic.

What he found confounded me. There was a hole in my left leg filled with pebbles. The pebbles and my immune system had coagulated the blood in the hole so I hadn't bled very much. What was worse to me, however, was the shock. I still couldn't stop shaking. He gave me a sedative.

After what seemed like a very, very long time, my body began returning to something like normal. The doctor and my personal nurse extracted all the pebbles, applied a bacterial disinfectant, and bandaged me up so I could walk.

My wonderful nurse took me home and put me to bed. About midday of the following day, I felt as right as rain. I received a call from the insurance company and they wanted to settle, of course. I told them that all I wanted was a new motorcycle, the same model as my old one, and to pay the clinic fee for my treatment, which was really minimal. (I only saw the doctor one more time and he gave me the thumbs up.)

From that accident I learned a couple of very important lessons, which have transcended the rest of my life. Regardless of what you do, stuff happens you can't control and you can't prepare for everything, regardless of what the Boy Scouts tell you. Also, more importantly, friends are essential and life without them is not only lonely, but can be life-threatening. So: be good to your friends!

# Skana, a Killer Whale

Skana was an adult killer whale which resided at the Vancouver Public Aquarium in Stanley Park, British Columbia. During the 1970s, she resided there for several years. While attending the University of Washington for two weekends each month, I would drive up to the aquarium and watch the belugas, orcas and dolphins they maintained.

I finally caught up with Gil Hewlett, a biologist that worked with the aquarium, and Dr. Murray Newman, the curator. In Dr. Newman's office, he had mounted on a wall a nearly six-foot-long narwhal tusk (the legendary unicorn horn), the first I had ever seen, and I was much impressed when he let me handle it.

During a couple weeks, I got to know him personally and he and Gil allowed me access to Skana, which, at the time, was residing in a back pool of the aquarium, away from the public. Gil and Dr. Newman found out that I was working with young orcas at the Seattle Marine Aquarium and they didn't feel there was much to worry about if I swam with Skana and did some underwater photography with her. I felt very privileged because she was going to be the first adult orca whale with which I had ever had a real close encounter.

I wrote a formal program through my science cetacean research project, Dolphin Marine Research, and handed it to Dr. Newman and Gil Hewlett. They liked my presentation and we set up the rendezvous for my next free weekend. I hot-footed it up to the aquarium with my scuba and a rented underwater camera.

My time in the pool with her was to reveal some of the most interesting behavior I have ever personally witnessed.

While I was observing her, I noticed that there were herring in the water, one of the fish that is less expensive than salmon and easier to use for training purposes. For a while, I just stayed by the side of the pool, dangling my flippers in the water so she could get used to my presence. She spy-hopped several times at first to get a good look at me and then came over to the side of the pool and lay on her side, eyeing me intently.

I showed her the camera and let her touch it with her big, round, shiny black rostrum. A little later, I slipped into the water with the camera and circled around her to let her get used to me in the pool. So far, everything was going pretty much as I thought it would.

Then she got moody.

Some people actually believe animals do not have emotions. They are wrong, dead wrong. Humans have thirty-two different emotions, some of them diametrically opposed, like love and hate. Animals probably have a number of different kinds of these emotions and they express them well. One simply needs to know how to read these emotions, something I have gotten very good at over the years.

The closer I got to Skana, the more agitated she became and after a little while she wanted to continue feeding and I was in her way. As I was getting some great underwater shots of her feeding on the herring, I wasn't in any hurry to leave her pool.

She jaw clapped at me. I not only saw her do it, I heard the sound coming out of her massive jaws. It was my first warning to get out of the pool and not be so dumb-headed.

Within five minutes, something more major happened; it was my second warning. She pushed me against the side of her pool and held me there, her rostrum against my chest. I couldn't move up, down, or sidewise. I just held the camera in one hand, away from my body.

Fortunately, I was wearing scuba because she held me underwater for a full three minutes, longer than I could have held my breath without scuba.

At first, I tensed up and tried to squirm out of her grasp, but then I relaxed. She could apparently feel me and she backed up, letting me go. I swam to the opposite side of the pool, but still didn't get out of her territory. She started feeding again. By the time she had nearly finished, there were only a few herring drifting around the pool.

I was still in close contact with her. And she didn't like it. She showed it by coming over and biting me on my left hand, the hand that, at the moment, didn't have a firm grip on the other side of the camera. I could feel the pressure on my knuckles all the way through the neoprene glove I was wearing.

Well, that last warning was straightforward enough that I exited the pool with the camera. I took off my neoprene glove and looked for damage to my hand. Aside from a little redness, there wasn't even a bite mark. If she had been a dog, it would have been a different story, because canines can hang on and bite deeply.

Skana taught me a lot of different things that day in her pool. Firstly, orcas have terrific control over their emotions, but they do express them freely. Secondly, like humans, orca have degrees of emotion, which can escalate. Thirdly, orcas have tremendous control over their mouth and teeth, something I didn't expect at all.

She didn't want to hurt me, she just wanted me out of her pool while she was feeding. No other diver I talked to at the aquarium had ever experienced her warnings. I was the apparently the first, and it was all due to my insistence that I be near her while she was feeding.

I know of killer whales who have become fed up with certain trainers and have expressed deep emotion toward them. One orca at the defunct Japanese Gardens Aquarium in Los Angeles completely demolished the training platform from which a trainer tried to mis-train the animal in his care. The orca was so confused that she lashed out in the only way she knew she could effectively communicate. The trainer finally did get the message, as I did.

And finally, there are trainers who have been killed through their own negligence. Orcas, especially young orcas, like to play. They are robust creatures and they do not realize how fragile human beings are compared to themselves. One young lady, who was an Olympic quality swimmer, at the now defunct Sealand Aquarium in Victoria, Canada, was drowned by three young orcas, one young male in particular named

Tillicum. She had just finished a training session with them and simply fell into the pool with the playful animals. She was toyed with like a wet rubber ball until she expired. Years later, at Seaworld, Tillicum killed another trainer. I seriously suspect it was another play-oriented mistake.

You simply do not make mistakes when training animals that have more power and endurance than you do.

# Packrats and Rattlesnakes

Gold mines are features of the Met-how Valley and I explored as many of them as I could find. Packrats and rattlesnakes sometimes inhabit these mines and one needs to be wary of them at all times. These borrow loving creatures can hide in the most unlikely places. Encounter one at the wrong time and you can be in serious trouble.

One winter day we were filming a motion picture called "The Wish" in a mine. The mine itself was owned by two old gentlemen who didn't live in the Met-how, but mined it more or less as a hobby. The mine had been tunneled through in two levels, a horizontal level and another level that angled upwards about twenty feet from the entrance. That part was short and had caved in at one point in time, leaving rubble and big timbers all over the lower floor.

When I went into the mine in the early spring the first time, exploring it as a potential movie location, I was wearing a metal helmet attached to which was a carbide lamp, the kind underground miners have used for decades. About a quarter of the way in, I saw a small pair of eyes shining back at me. A large packrat had made her nest in the rubble.

I am sure she was happy to live there, but very unhappy to see me. When I went slowly over and approached her, she stood her ground and hissed at me like a snake. She wouldn't let me go deeper into the mine that I had heard was probably 1200 or so feet longer than where I was standing. I stood my ground, too, not wanting to approach her closer, but not wanting to leave, either.

For the better part of fifteen minutes I tried to show her I wasn't there to hurt her. Finally, I think she had enough of me. I thought she was charging, maybe a bluff charge as bears sometimes do, when she came straight at me. I held my ground.

When I didn't back up, I guess she decided to give up, because she rushed right past my legs and out toward the entrance. When I examined her nest, I found there were no young in it. That is why she gave up; she had nothing worthwhile to protect. If there had been young in the nest, her hormones would have insisted that she chase me away, maybe even bite me to give me a message. As a result, I explored the mine to its maximum length and it did become part of my movie.

Another mine I explored was the Eureka mine. This one proved to be even more exciting. The time was late fall.

You never know what you will find in an old abandoned mine. The Eureka entrance is merely a haphazard hole cut into the side of a mountain. The cut goes downward and then straightens out horizontally. The entrance hole isn't as big as the entrance in the previous mine I told you about.

The reason the Met-how mines aren't bigger is that the gold that came out of them was sparse for the tedious work involved. There is gold in them, but the gold takes a lot of work to process out of the surrounding rock. One might as well be a rancher or a farmer for the wealth that comes out of one. However, in the glory days of these Met-how mines, the 1890s, there weren't any ranchers or farmers, just Indians and settlers getting settled onto new territory.

The late fall day I got on my knees to enter the mine and slid through the opening I will never forget. Maybe twenty feet into it through the light of my carbide lamp, I saw something slithering and brown; it wasn't just one rattlesnake, it was a rattlesnake ball.

For those of you who have never seen one, it is quite amazing. Many kinds of snakes den up for the winter in balls in cold territory like the Met-how Valley. They use what minimal heat is in their body to keep each other from freezing to death.

Caves, large burrows, and abandoned mines are especially suited for hibernating snakes curled into balls. Many animals that you think of as hibernating don't actually deep sleep. They can be easily awakened. I once crawled into a bear hibernation cave and found a young black bear. When I stroked his course fur, he almost woke up, giving me a start. You can imagine how fast I crawled backward out of his little cave.

Back to the rattlesnakes . . . I didn't want to get to close to them, of course. Even though one animal might cause you trouble, a group of animals can be deadly and I was a score of miles from any kind of medical help.

Unfortunately, the light and the heat from my carbide lamp, and maybe even my own body heat, too, was enough to awaken the ball. From something barely moving, the ball seemed to disintegrate in front of my eyes. I began backing up.

That was a problem, because there was a lot of fallen rock everywhere and I could have easily tripped over any large chunk of it and within seconds had rattlesnakes all over me. That couldn't end up well for me.

I like reptiles, but not that much. I couldn't turn off the carbide lamp, either, because I was too deep into the mine and wouldn't have been able to find my way out.

I then remembered what an old grizzly bear hunter had told me one time about brown bears. "Unless you have a really powerful gun, don't even try to kill a grizzly. If you wound him, you'll just make him mad and he'll come after you. If he's already too close to you, shoot the ground near his feet. Grizzly's have a powerful sense of smell. When the dust rises up around his feet, it will confuse him and he will stand up on his hind legs to investigate you, but he won't charge you. Then you just back away."

That sounded like good advice for this situation as more and more rattlesnakes were coming my way in the semi-darkness. I started kicking up dust with my feet as I backtracked; more and more of it rose from the ground. I rubbed my hand against the ceiling of the cave and more and more dust came down. I kept back stepping, trying to fog the snakes' chemo-reception as well as their eyesight. Soon there was so much dust in the air, I couldn't see snakes, either. I kept back stepping, a little faster now.

I never thought a wall of dust would ever be any kind of protection, but this wall seemed to be doing the job as I neared the cave entrance and could finally see bright light behind me.

Quicker than I came in, I exited the Eureka mine and breathed a huge sigh of relief when I smelled pine trees again. I didn't hang around to see if any of the rattlesnakes came out behind me.

# Staking Mineral Rights

One of my first paying jobs in the Met-how Valley was placing small documents inside canisters on hillsides, staking out the mineral mining interests of Quintana Minerals, a Canadian-based company. Occasionally, new documents need to replace old documents. It was my job to replace new, updated ones for old ones that had been originally placed years and years before.

I loved hiking, and getting paid for hiking around the magnificent Met-how Valley seemed like a heavenly job. For days at a time, I would hike up and down parts of the sixty-mile-long Met-how looking for these canisters. I would always be home in the evening after dark, so nothing about the wildlife of the Met-how scared me much. A few times I could feel a cougar watching me, a few times I could see white-tailed deer and I came upon mule deer rather constantly.

Once I ran into an old black bear and yelled out the Salish Indian equivalent phase at him of "Go home grandpa!" That bear turned tail and ran away. As a result, I was pretty confident I wasn't going to be gobbled up by anything normal. Sasquatches I wasn't so sure about, but I had heard from locals that they are nocturnal anyway.

Then came the day I had to post Quintana's updated documents in those cylinders around a pond. Ponderosa trees were here and there. Beneath several of the ponderosas was a canister nailed to a stick about three feet tall. Below the stick was a rattlesnake about two and a half to three feet long.

When I came near one, its tail would start buzzing and the snake would coil up, as if to strike. I could tell they weren't happy to see me.

In fact, it was probably the first time any of those particular snakes had ever seen a human being. Such reptiles can live up to twenty years and the original documents had been placed in the cylinders in the 1920s.

To a rattlesnake, anything tall is a threat. Lots of creatures eat rattlesnakes. I have tried cooking a few and I've found out that I can live without them.

To not place the document in the canister meant that Quintana could lose their rights to the minerals in that location, and who knows what might have been in the area. Certainly I didn't.

Mineral companies collect core samples to find out what is beneath the soil in what substrate and I had seen dozens of such core samples from areas throughout their Met-how mineral rights areas. There was absolutely no question that I needed to place the new documents in the canisters where the rattlesnakes were.

Now, for those of you that aren't familiar with rattlesnakes, let me state this: they can spring jump at least their own length. So, if you see a rattlesnake, don't toy with it, especially if it's coiled. There are very few animals that attack rattlesnakes and get away with it. Only the badger and the wolverine come to mind.

What was my option? Nothing really, but I did know more than a few things about western rattlesnakes . . . they don't like rocks for one thing. And if you have a long branch with a V-end in it, you can sometimes gently pick up a snake and place it somewhere else. This, however, I wouldn't advise unless you know how.

Between rocks and a V-branch, I was able to convince ten of the rattlesnakes to move to other locations. I was absolutely exhausted after about an hour and a half of this and I still had a long way to go to place all the other documents for the day.

That evening I came home to the old rural farmhouse I was renting near the small town of Mazama in the northern Met-how Valley. Wouldn't you know it? I ran into yet another rattlesnake. This one was under my car in the driveway. When it started rattling the buttons in its tail, I jumped about four feet high in three directions, not knowing exactly where it was in the near darkness. Fortunately, no snake bit me that day, but if one had, I would have been again very far away from any sort of help.

Oh, and I didn't tell you either about the black bear that decided to raid the beehives that were on my front porch. (I always entered the house from the side kitchen door.) The bear incident happened a few days later and I was almost furious enough to get into a fist fight with that marauding bear. Almost. As it was, he got away with nearly all the honey my domesticated bees made that summer . . . honey I was planning to use myself.

# Disassembling an Antique Barn

The style of barn that friends and I tore down that one sometimes finds in the Met-how Valley. They can be dangerous places, especially if they are ready to fall down by themselves during the next snowstorm.

Old barns have intrigued me since I was a youngster, probably because my grandfather built one on his farm in 1908-1909 in Puyallup, Washington. Barns, for those of you who have never had the pleasure of playing in one, are fascinating places with distinctive smells all their own. They take on the smell of the hay and grain that is stored there, of the animals they protect from inclement weather, and the smell of the mice, rats, birds, and insects that habitually make their nests in the barns. Believe it or not, the composite smell is not unpleasant; at least, for me it wasn't. The sweet smell of hay and corn stalks, feed for the cattle and the horse, usually overwhelmed all the other smells except the urine and cow and horse pies that were deposited in the trough of the barn daily.

The loft of my grandfather's barn was particularly intriguing because it was a bit like a tree house. One had to climb a handmade wooden ladder in order to get up the ten feet or so above the first floor. Then you could luxuriate in the hay as long as you wanted to. I kissed my first girlfriend in the hay in a place exactly like that loft, so it obviously has even more special memories for me.

Northwest US barns generally have steep roofs to allow snow to slide off easily, generally because (in the early 1900s) barns were unheated. Things have gotten pretty sophisticated more recently, but the barn I was about to help friends disassemble was an unheated, larger timber post and beam barn, the kind my grandfather had built. The roofline was a good thirty feet off the ground.

My friends had been disassembling the fir lumber barn for nearly a week. By the 1970s, the barn boards on old barns had turned many different colors—yellows, greens, reds, browns, and black in places around knotholes—so this kind of thick wood, aged wood was very desirable for interior decorating. Just one wall of interior barn board could transform a room, and my friends and I were definitely into that sort of thing. I had just built my own house several years before (1974 -1975) this tragic incident entirely out of recycled lumber. Old farmers were eager to have old structures torn down so they could be replaced by newer, more modern buildings; students of history like me were even more eager to tear them down for the materials.

And so it was that I found myself thirty and more feet high, taking apart the roof of an antique barn. All that remained of the structure were four skeleton walls and I was standing on the highest ribs of one of the walls. The only large beam left was the one that connected the two opposite sides of the walls. I had attached myself to one end of the 10" X 10" beam and a friend of mine was at the other end.

Below both of us were the miscellaneous leavings of the rest of the disassembly, broken boards, ten-inch long hand made nails and spikes, tar paper, and all sorts of other materials that had been in the barn for a very long time. There was also old hay scattered here and there.

The one really fortunate thing about the disassembly that day was that we had picked an autumn to lay waste to this barn and the weather was terrific—still hot, dry, and sunny.

With a hammer, I pulled out the last two long spikes holding the ridge beam in place on my side and they fell to the ground. I waved to my friend on the other side of the beam. He had pulled his two out as well, and he waved back. We were ready to lift the beam from its V-shaped holding areas on each wall and drop the beam into the bottom of the barn.

We began to lift the very heavy beam from its cradle. Somehow, the beam caught the clothes I was wearing and my end of the beam started falling. So did I . . . I fell all thirty plus feet and hit the wooden hay covered floor of the barn. The beam landed right beside me; fortunately, not on top of me.

I lay there for awhile, dazed. Everyone gathered around me. They said I looked dead. I heard one of them say, "Don't move him. If he isn't dead, he might have a spinal injury or something else. Someone go phone a doctor."

After I could finally open my eyes, I saw my friends gathered all around me. I saw some other things, too. When I turned my head to right, I saw that my head had barely missed a ten inch spike that was sticking straight upwards out of a broken board. When I turned my head to the left, I saw that my head had missed another ten inch spike that was sticking straight upwards out of another broken board. How I missed either one of them is some sort of miracle.

When I tried to move, I found that it was difficult. I had dislocated my left shoulder from its socket; the same shoulder I had dislocated during my gynamstics "eagle" maneuver on the high bar.

"Are you alright?" someone asked me.

"I think so," I said, trying to put the best face on it, and also not trying to act completely stupid. Falling from my perch had been stupid enough. "But my shoulder is hurting. I can't move it without a lot of pain. I think I'd better go see a doctor. The beam is down. I'll bet now you guys won't have trouble taking down the rest of the walls. I'm leaving it up to you," I joked. I tried moving my shoulder one way and then another. It hurt even worse than before.

"So . . . who is going to drive me down to Pateros. I don't think I can drive myself right now."

One of the girls volunteered and in a 1989 Volkswagen Bug we made our way along a rocky, hilly country road; every bump was painful for me; my stomach was a mess and I wanted to throw up every time we hit a bump or went over a hill; I nearly passed out twice before we drove the thirty mile distance necessary to get me to the emergency room of the hospital. My driver was steadfast, however, and got me there before any more damage resulted.

It took a team of doctors all day to mend me what with having to take X-rays, to maneuver my shoulder back into its socket, and then to wrap my shoulder tightly and make me a brace.

I took a bus home, but despite the pain reliever I had been given, the shoulder still ached like Billy-be-damned.

It was quite a surprise for my father, who at that time owned The Last Trading Post in Winthrop, Washington, and for whom I was working part-time. The next day I tried to work, but it was too difficult for me. Even turning and trying to pick up something from the floor was impossible; trying to wrap something for a customer was out of the question. Even making change took way more time than should have been necessary.

"You're pretty useless, son," my father said jokingly, about ready to pat me on the arm. "I think you ought to take a couple months of vacation."

I turned away protectively. "I'd be up to that," I replied. "Where do you think I should go?"

"You have that doctor friend in Santa Cruz. I think you should go see him."

"That would be good. I haven't really saved up much money though," I said honestly.

He gave me a couple hundred bucks for my past salary and use of his motor home, an American Clipper.

"It's nearly new…don't wreck it," he said before I left.

"It'll be all right. I drive with my right hand," I said.

"You owe me. . . big time," he added.

I agreed I would pay off the use of the motor home in time spent cashiering in the store when I got back.

I spent the next three months playing chess with my eighty-year old doctor friend and visiting sea lions at Santa Cruz, California. I learned quite a lot about sea lions, gray whales who migrate through the area, sea otters at Monterey, and about fishes at the Monterey Bay Aquarium. I had the time of my life.

What I learned from this episode was that accidents will happen to you, no matter how careful you are. For your own mental health, you've just got to make the best of the results of them, or, as one friend of mine once said, "If life hands you lemons, make lemonaide . . . with sugar. It's all in the lemons and the sweetener."

# Climbing Silver Star

Living in the Met-how Valley, a person has the opportunity to climb mountains, none of which are more than about 9,000 feet tall. On the top of those mountains are registers placed there by the U.S. Forest Service, so that when a person does reach the top, s(he) can sign the register to document that s(he) has been there.

Silver Star Mountain is one of the most climbable mountains in the North Cascades National Park. I climbed its west face, possibly the only person who has ever done so and when I was resting, I signed the register. This is the story of that precarious climb and how I nearly lost my life there.

People say that mountain climbing is near the top of harzardous things to do and I believe it, because unexpected things can happen at unexpected times. No matter how careful you are, no matter how well prepared you are, no matter how nice the weather is, a mountain's environment can change quickly and radically.

My little group of a half dozen mountaineers started out on Highway Number 20 on a beautiful sunny day in July. The weather was hot and dry, but there was still a nice big nesting glacier near the top of the mountain. The very top of Silver Star was seeable and void of snow. I figured it ought to be an easy climb considering other moutains I had climbed. No ropes were necessary, no petons, for attaching lines so our group was minimally clothed in light pants and shirts.

It was to be a long day hike with lunch or an early dinner at the top. Hopefully, we would be at our respective cars, going back home, by late evening. No bears or cougars were expected to jump out at us so we didn't bring a pistol, just an ice axe for each of us to get across the glacier. We were also wearing crampons on our shoes to traverse it. Below the glacier was a waterfall and below it were jaggged rocks that had fallen down the waterfall over the years.

We prepared ourselves and hiked down off of Highway Number 20 and then we crossed the river. We found deer trails heading up the mountain and followed them until we ran out of trails, which ended just below the glacier. We kept hiking up the glacier until we were nearly to the top–the smallest part of the glacier. Then we carefully and methodically started crossing it. Most everyone had gone across, I was the last to do so. Unfortunately for me, I was the last to do so.

The glacier in the direct sunlight had been getting slicker and slicker so that when I crossed, I slipped on the ice. Flat on my stomach and sliding down the glacier at a speed that kept increasing, I couldn't get the spikes on my crampons to contact the ice. I knew that death on the rocks was imminent at the bottom of the waterfall. My mind quickly started churning through options of how to slow my speed.

Nothing made any sense except to use my ice axe, but at the speed I was going, I couldn't get it into the ice. I kept sliding down closer and closer toward the waterfall.

In one last desperate attempt with the ice axe, I turned the point around and pushed myself off the ice. When I came down, the point of the ice axe stuck in the ice and I pressed my entire chest and body weight against it. My body weight pressed the axe point deeper and deeper into the glacier as I moved closer to the waterfall. I began slowing down and was able to catch my breath.

Within a few feet of the end of the glacier, the start of the waterfall, I stopped. I still had a problem though . . . if I wasn't able to stand up and walk across the last, widest point of the waterfall, I would still fall the fifty or so feet off the glacier onto the rocks below.

For several minutes I remained as still as possible, trying to figure out how I was going to stand up with the ice axe still embedded in the slippery glacier. I thought I couldn't abandon it, because I needed it to get across. Having gymnastic training turned out again to be a very important facility. I muscled my entire body above the ice axe and turned in an exaggerated arc so I could plant my crampons into the ice.

Slowly, very slowly I rose up, one hand on the glacier and the other on the ice axe.

I was looking into the depths of the waterfall and getting a bit dizzy from the sight, so I closed my eyes and let my senses do the rest. Even more slowly I got to my feet and stood there, adjusting my balance. I left the ice axe where it was. One foot at a time, a few inches at a time, I crossed that glacier to the encouraging shouts of my fellow mountaineers.

The rest of the climb was a breeze and I had a very late, well deserved lunch with them.

What did I learn from this adventure? One never knows what prior training will be beneficial to you throughout your life. For me, it was gymnastics and though I never won an award for being an all around gymnast, on this occasion the training saved my life. Thank God for gym teachers!

# Dead Man's Canyon

Fishing can be an amazing experience and this trip was to prove nearly disastrous. The date was October 15, 1985 when a friend of mine and I set out for a heavenly fishing spot called Lost Lakes, a series of three small alpine lakes. Each lake fed into the next and each one was fed by melting glacial snow, which had not yet come for the fall season.

We weren't expecting snow so early in the season. Usually around the North Cascades Mountains the first snow comes about November 1st, but it doesn't stick. The real snow comes after November 15th and it starts piling up like crazy.

It isn't unusual to have a foot of snow every day after that. One year, we had a five-foot overnight snowfall and a local man died of a heart attack the next day while shoveling it.

In order to get to Lost Lakes one has to set out from Highway Number 20, the North Cascades Highway of Washington State, the most northerly route east to west, west to east. You start out south of Silver Star Mountain, go down a steep embankment, cross a river, and head up a switchback that is several miles long.

It takes a good part of the day to reach the saddle between two mountains, the only place that leads to Lost Lakes. Some people do it by horses and I understand why after hiking all that way with about thirty pounds of gear and a little food on my back.

Our plan was to hike in, fish all the next day, clean the fish we caught, and then hike out the next day to get home. Great plan, we thought.

The front part of the plan—the hike in part and the fish all the next day part— went just as we expected. At the first of the Lost Lakes (the smallest one) we didn't really catch much so we moved on to the next lake. Not much was biting there, either.

When we came to the largest of the three alpine lakes, I couldn't throw my spinner in fast enough. Every time it hit the water, I caught a cutthroat trout. Each one I landed was the same size—fourteen inches, the perfect eating size.

As I examined the stomach of some of the fish, I found that they had eaten nothing for a long time except algae at the bottom of the lake and a few mosquitos. All the fish in the lake had apparently matured to the same size. That was a revelation.

I was years later to read a science paper by Edward O. Wilson, the top biologist at Harvard University, that concluded the size of the enclosure determines the size of the inhabitant. He was apparently right. No fish in that lake seemed to be over fourteen inches long.

We took a break from fishing and pitched our pup tents and got our campfire ready in case the weather changed from being so nice to being inclement, something that can happen quickly in the mountains. We gathered enough loose firewood in the area that the fire would stay lit in case some bear, wolf, bobcat, or other inquisitive mammal came by, drawn by the smell of the fish we were catching. I had already seen a fisher (a type of large fish-eating weasel) in the first lake hunting his lunch.

By the time the afternoon was done, I had caught fifty trout and my partner had caught about an equal number. Since this was our entire winter fish supply, which would be frozen when we got home the next day, we were over-the-moon pleased with our catching results.

Around supper time, we ate a few of the trout. They were delicious, especially in that mountain lake setting. It took us nearly half way to mid-night to gut the rest.

This is a description of the fish we caught. A cutthroat trout's body color is highly variable. Its back may be steel gray to olive-green; its sides may be yellow-brown with red or pink along the belly. Slash marks on either side of the throat beneath the lower jaw may be yellow, crimson-red or orange. Fins are a uniform color with no white tips. Scattered spots are usually round and black, more closely grouped towards the tail. (The fish we caught were all these colorations with lots of spots.)

There are teeth on back of its tongue. A cutthroat may even hybridize with a rainbow trout. Cutthroat's are native to Washington State. Most of the adults are about fourteen inches long, the size we caught.

By the time we had stuffed the fish carefully in our pack sacks, the pack sacks were already heavy and we still would need to put our sleeping bags, tents, and cooking paraphenalia in, around, and on top of the cleaned fish. I tell you, I wasn't looking forward to leaving with over sixty-plus pounds on my back, but I sure wasn't leaving any of them either.

A star-shot night appeared through a clear sky and we two talked about all kinds of things around our campfire. The Milky Way and all sorts of constellations were unsurpassed in their beauty. We couldn't have asked for nicer weather.

It's really amazing how many stars are in our heavens. It is calculated that there are over 100 million of them in our Milky Way Galaxy and no one yet knows how many planets. I believe you can see every one of them from the high altitude of the Lost Lakes area with no obscuring smog around you.

We stuffed the pack sacks into our sleeping tents with us and the smoothly flowing fresh night air lulled us both into deep sleep. If any animal did come around, we didn't hear it. Neither one of us woke until morning.

The freezing, extreme winter-like sight beholding us when we awoke was completely unexpected and completely hazardous. Snow everywhere was knee deep. There wasn't an animal track in it. Wow, what a difference from the day before when we had hiked in. And not only that, but there was a deep, penetrating fog everywhere. We couldn't see ten feet in any direction around us.

We already knew we were in trouble. We took down our tents and packed our equipment around the fish, which we found were already frozen to the core, each one a little heavier than the day we had caught them.

With very heavy packs on our backs, we started in the direction of home . . . what we thought was the direction of home. We had no compass with us. As I said in another story, in eastern Washington one doesn't ordinarily need a compass as trails feed into each other and are usually marked in some way. Our route hadn't been marked, but we at least knew that we needed to go out the same direction as we had come into Lost Lakes. And that was the problem.

When you have that much fog and that much snow around you, you have a difficult time knowing if you are traveling in any right direction. You also have a difficult enough time knowing if you are traveling uphill or down hill.

For hours, we trekked through the snow. We thought we should be reaching the saddle between the mountains, our exit to the long switchback to get us back home. If you haven't done it, trekking through ankle deep slow is extremely tedious work . . . real work. Our legs were getting more and more tired with every step. First, my companion would break trail and then I would break trail, the hardest part of walking through knee-deep snow. I admit my partner on this journey was much better at it than I was.

Both of us had snowshoes at home and were proficient in their use, but neither of us had brought a pair. Because of all the great weather all the week before, we certainly didn't think we would need them on this fishing trip. There are a lot of ifs in life. If only we had brought them.

After another twenty minutes of fighting the snow and fog, we took a long needed rest. We thought over our situation.

Were we going the right direction after all?

We still hadn't found the saddle between the mountains and we were getting desperate and tired. If we were going downhill rather than uphill, we would eventually end up at Dead Man's Canyon, a box canyon with only one way in and one way out. We might end up like the 1860s California Donner Party–bogged down in snow with no place to go. Eating each other after eating the trout didn't seem like a good idea even then.

After deliberation, we decided that our legs were so exhausted that they could no longer tell if we were going uphill or down hill. I suggested that, despite our extreme tiredness, that we backtrack until we knew we were going uphill. Something in the back of my mind told me that if we kept going in the same direction we had been going, we were likely to be in really serious straits.

Somehow from deep within, we pulled out more strength. We had reached our second wind hours before. We were necessarily going on complete reserves now, another plateau, one that we didn't even know existed. Neither of us had ever heard of a third wind.

Step by hard step, pain shooting through each of our legs, we backtracked.

When we started falling down every other step, we knew we were going uphill. The packs on our backs felt heavier than at any time before. We even thought about discarding them and all our easily won fish, coming back for them at some later date.

We trudged on, one tedious, deliberate step after another, taking more and more rest periods. The snow started coming down all over again, covering our past tracks. The fog was relentless, never lifting an inch in any direction. In fact, it seemed to be getting worse the higher we climbed. Now we could barely see each other and we were only a few feet apart.

The ten-mile hike from Lost Lakes back to the North Cascades Highway was starting to feel like 100 miles and we had yet to reach the saddle.

In another half hour, we actually did find the saddle between the two mountains, but now the snow was up to our waists. Could conditions get any worse?

Unbelievably, the answer was, " Yes!"

The way down the switchback was also covered by snow, but not so deep. The heavy packs on our backs kept making us slip and slid down that steep switchback. Not only our legs, but now our knees were quickly wearing out. I fell down and rolled several feet, got back up, and kept falling down.

We took another badly needed rest break.

For two more hours, nearly beyond our limits of endurance, we kept going down that switchback until we reached the river. There was an old black bear there to greet us and he smelled frozen fish. His nose was in the air and he was sniffing rapidly.

Great . . . and neither one of us had the energy to fight him off if he decided to take our fish. We armed ourselves with rocks from the riverbed just in case.

The bear apparently knew what we were up to, or, he simply wasn't hungry enough to attack. He looked fat, as if he had been gorging on huckleberries, insects, and other things black bears love. He looked fat enough, in fact, that he could easily have been looking for a den somewhere in which to hibernate for the winter. At any rate, thankfully he left us alone as we crossed the river.

Uphill, far uphill, we both saw the car that we had parked on the Cascade Highway, the vehicle that would take us home, if we could get to it. Snow on this side of the mountains wasn't nearly as deep as we had already trekked through. We were delighted and took yet another of our long breaks.

The last uphill leg of the journey was the easiest, because we found an established deer trail. We did reach the car and with all the fish and all our gear intact.

What a battle! It was with ourselves, the weather, and the long, tedious hike. I decided never to hike to Long Lakes again in late fall; it was just too dangerous. If we hadn't decided to back track, we would never have found our way back home. We would have been in Dead Man's Canyon.

This was all before the age of cell phones. Nowadays, if you are lost and someone is trying to find you, all you need to do is turn on your phone and the GPS on it will allow your rescuers to find you. That is, if your phone is properly charged.

Isn't technology wonderful?

So, what did I learn from this experience? I learned that a human being can go beyond whatever limits s(he) thought was possible from past experience. There is not only a second wind, another plateau, but also a third wind, an even higher energy plateau, if one truly reaches deep enough within oneself to use it.

Necessity is not only the mother of invention, necessity is what can drive a human being to their absolute personal limits in the worst possible situation.

# The Executive Monkey

From all the past decisions I have made to this point in my life, including all the near disasters I have survived from, becoming an executive monkey was the worst decision of my life. It was the one that most nearly killed me.

By late 1971, I was attending the University of Florida in an accelerated Master's/Ph.D program in the Speech Department and also working at the Marineland Research Laboratory when one day I got a call from my father. He was still living in the Met-how Valley of Washington State and had started a small business called The Last Trading Post. He needed help.

"I am dying," he said. "If you want to see me again, you had better come now. When I am gone, someone needs to run the business."

It was a hard decision to leave a life of academics to pursue a life of retail, because I was good at academics and I love to learn, but because it was probably the last time I could experience being with a father. I did go and help him and left college behind.

When I arrived back in Winthrop, I hadn't intended to stay, but dad was right. He was sickly and needed at least part-time help in his new small store, so I did stay. He wanted to remodel the place and make the interior look turn-of-the-century like the rest of the town. So, yes, I helped him do it. We laid down a maple hardwood floor, put up beams, and generally had a good time doing it. With his Navy pension, dad bought some merchandise for the store and opened his business in our tourist-related town.

Before I got to Winthrop, in fact, while I was in St. Augustine, my father had been the President of the Winthrop Chamber of Commerce when the entire town decided to remodel from a 1950s hunting and fishing- looking town into a "new" turn-of-the-century frontier-looking town.

The facelifts of the buildings were simply remarkable owing to the talents of an architect named Robert Jorgenson, who had previously redesigned the oldish town of Leavenworth, Washington, into a Bavarian village.

After a few months of working with dad, he was actually looking better, way better than I had expected and we had a few more good months together. His wife, still a young woman of thirty nine could have taken over the store if my father did die, so I planned to go back to Florida.

However, life is often full of unpleasant surprises and something else unexpected happened. His wife, my step-mother, Marilyn, died of a very fast spreading incurable kind of cancer. What a shocker! This left my two step-brothers without the support of a mother and my father in his deteriorating condition could barely handle two boys, six years and four years old.

I filled in, although I still thought my life would be in academia, probably as a professor of speech or as a research scientist.

After a year of working with him, my father looked pretty good to me, but he still had a drinking problem and he smoked about six packs of cigarettes a day. Even in those days of mass advertising of "cancer sticks" I knew that smoking couldn't be good for him. He had smoked since he was sixteen years old, heavily from about twenty one, and he was now nearly forty eight.

In his last year, I got him to go to Alcholics Anonymous and he did stop drinking. He became a new man for that year, a lot more mellow and loving to his two young sons.

As my father's illness progressed, he found he could no longer handle the store, which was getting more and more traffic. I bought the store from him and settled in. I gave up my academic career for a business model and ran the Last Trading Post, sometimes at a profit, sometimes at break-even, but never in the red.

All the while, I was in a terrific common law marriage with the same woman, a terrific and honest business partner. I could not have run the business without her.

The trading post business was highly seasonal. Snow fell from November through March and so nearly closed both highways leading from other parts of Washington State to Winthrop. Usually in the middle of November, Highway Number 20, the most northernly route through Washington State, did close itself through huge snow slides and it became too costly for the county to keep the road open.

Since there were only about 2,000 people living in the entire Methow Valley, my clientelle was completely limited and I catered mostly to the summer and spring and early fall tourist trade. Winter and early spring I dedicated myself to writing novels and screenplays, playing chess with members of the community, and involving myself in civic causes designed to make the community an even better place to do business. Several years, I used my late fall-winters to go back to Florida and train dolphins again.

I couldn't get my father to stop smoking. By then, every cell in his body had been infiltrated with nicotene and other noxious materials and that is what actually killed him. One evening, one of his lungs exploded from all the tar that had accumulated in it. He was only forty-nine.

I lived in Winthrop for twenty nine years and adored the place. There was so much to do and so many different venues to do it through. Over the years we filmed commercials, videos, and parts of movies in and around Winthrop, Washington and Okanogan County.

The trading post business continued to be a lot of fun and different every day. I would go to farm auctions, buy a bunch of stuff, and sell it to tourists. They loved the store and came by time and again. I did a lot of commercials in those days and even flew to Philadelphia to be on a game show hosted by Bill Cosby. I had a great time and brought back some prize money.

The business was so much fun, in fact, that I had excellent health and never needed to visit a doctor for twenty-eight years. I never got so much as a cold.

During my twenty-nine retail years, I accumulated a bunch of stuff, properties, a forty foot by sixty foot, two story warehouse and owned both The Last Trading Post outright and about half of a large restaurant called The Winthrop Palace. I say half, because I pumped enough money into that place that I owned half its equity.

Why am I detailing all this? I will get to it shortly.

Small towns are important. They can give you opportunities that you can get nowhere else, but you have to put your energy and soul into everything you do in a small town, because as much as any place else, people depend upon you. Over the years, I became part of so many different things, people started calling my "Mr. Winthrop." A lot of people deserved that title.

Hunting and fishing were, and still are, two of the main economic generators for the four towns in the Methow Valley. South to north they are Methow, Twisp, Winthrop, and Mazama.

As you have discovered in previous stories, wildlife is abundant in and around the Met-how Valley. I saw black bears frequently. They would be on my porch, in my back yard, on trails throughout the valley, but rarely in town, unless they were dead, killed by hunters during the hunting season. Once in town, however, I did find a young black bear in a wild apple tree down by the Met-how River. Forest rangers brought him down with a tranquilizer dart and carted him off into the nearby Pasayten Wilderness and let him go.

Cattle drives right through town are still a feature of Winthrop as local ranchers herd their animals to Forest Service pasture during the summer or to fields fresh with grass.

Just across the street from The Last Trading Post was the Winthrop Palace restaurant. At the time, it was the biggest restaurant in Okanogan County, Washington. This is where most of my headaches began—literally. When I took it over, my local banker tried to warn me, but I was too eager to operate the place, so I wasn't paying attention.

Party time was on main street, known to locals as Riverside Avenue. Over the years, I helped establish several major festivals—The Rhythm and Blues Festival, The Country Western Festival, Christmas at the End of the Road, Octoberwest, The Antique Auto Show, and a few more minor ones.

During such times, main street became a big, big stage and automobiles were not allowed (except during the Antique Auto Show, when nothing but antique cars were allowed.)

Because we were a mock western town, I designed a lot of mock gun fights for the summer tourist season. I also did a Dr. Sneezy Hacker routine where I sold "remedies" that could cure virtually anything. During those days, I was quite a ham, well-spoken, and the object of many TV commercials, some of which, amazingly, are still running more than a decade later.

There had been two previous times in my life when I had been affiliated with the restaurant industry. When I was in my second year at the University of Washington I was a busboy, a dishwasher and back-up cook. That is when my story about the cold January night occurred.

When I came to Winthrop the first time to visit my father, after I had earned my B.A. in Psychology from Central Washington University in Ellensburg, some 180 miles away, my father had bought into a restaurant—Sam's Place—the only other restaurant in Winthrop at the time.

Before I had left for Florida to become a research assistant, I had helped him run his restaurant. Anyway, I thought I knew restauranting pretty well, considering all the work I had done in two of them.

After twenty eight years in the trading post business, I had the best possible credit rating. So, what did I do then? I bought the failing Winthrop Palace.

Its previous owner was having trouble and as then president of the Winthrop Chamber of Commerce I knew our town desperately needed the Palace and as many restaurants as possible. At that time, the Palace was the only restaurant that could service two or more bus loads of people at the same time. By then, also we had already had two restaurants shut down and our tourists needed some big, easily accessible place to eat in.

I became the executive monkey, riding herd on over forty employees in two different kinds of business, right across the street from one another.

If you've never been an executive monkey, let me now explain what happens to you. Psychology experiments have shown over and over that the manager of others suffers the most damage, psychologically and physically. If I hadn't been so altruistic to the town, I guess I wouldn't have had to prove it to myself that it was true. (The executive monkey is sometimes also called the "fender executive," the one who takes the shit off the wheels.)

From the time I reopened the Palace in March to when I shut it down in December, it was a constant headache. For the first three weeks, I had stress-related diarrhea. My labor pool was severely restricted. My best cook was a cocaine addict. My partner, although financially supportive was a manic/depressive, and the forty employees did what they wanted, when they wanted, despite most of my instructions to the contrary. In short, the place was a disaster waiting to happen. One day our primary grill, an essential piece of equipment, blew up three times. The next day I replaced it.

Despite all its problems, the Palace building was beautiful and the food we served was delicious. It attracted a couple of bus loads of people every morning in the summer through fall so clientele wasn't a problem. It also attracted locals for breakfast, lunch and dinner, and I received compliments every day. We had wonderful bands on Thursday, Friday and Saturday nights and I actually liked running the place.

My partner said to me one day, "You had better start delegating and not doing everything yourself." But then she would leave or be in one of her manic/depressive moods.

She was quite right, of course. Up till then, my idea of leadership was to do everything by example, lead from the front. I had never expected someone to do something I wouldn't do myself. The problem in the restaurant was that everyone I hired let me do everything by myself. When you hire people, you expect them to do their best all the time; you don't expect to have to do their job for them.

The effects of my kind of leadership on my body became severe over the months. My blood pressure went up, I had head-aches most of the time, I could never get more than a couple of hours of sleep at night. I would talk in my sleep.

My dreams were filled with business, not relaxing as they should have been. I developed shingles, fiery red spots across my stomach and back brought on by the stress of running the business. There were some times when I simply wanted to go deep into the surrounding forest and just sit there, listening to the wildlife. But the many demands of the Palace kept me moving.

I maintained a really high-class bar in The Winthrop Palace, but to get away, Three- Fingered Jack's Saloon down the street, the legal saloon in the State of Washington, became my watering hole. Sometimes I just had to escape, because at The Palace there was always something pressing to do—take inventory of the brews we sold and the basic products we made into our meals, food to buy, employees to pay, and a thousand other things.

When I researched the financial structure of the restaurant business, I thought such a business made about ten percent net. Mine made only five percent, despite all the money it brought in and which I spent two or more hours every night counting. The rent on the business was high . . . $10,000 a month. And yes, as I say, it was very seasonal, so that it couldn't possibly make money in the late fall to early, early spring. Everything about that business seemed to be going against me and it showed.

By October, I felt a heart attack coming on.

When the business did shut down in early December, I moved to Florida again. Winthrop, as lovely and wonderful a town that it was, and especially the Winthrop Palace, had taken its emotional and physical toll on me.

Under doctor's orders, I rented a place on the Atlantic Ocean. There was a small bar a mile away from my house. Every day I would either walk the sand beach to the bar, have a drink, and swim back the mile to my house, or I would swim the mile to the bar, have a drink, and walk back on the sand beach to my house. It was quite a stict regime, but it did wonders for my body.

My blood pressure returned to normal, no more headaches, no more stress, no more worrying if I could pay my employees on time, no more setting up major festivals for the town during the busy tourist season, no more heavy demands on me from the town council.

There are people who can handle being the executive monkey and they become very good at it over time. Such people become the captains of industry and I respect them. But, it sure wasn't for me.

The Palace restaurant experience, however traumatic, did teach me valuable lessons . . . lessons in leadership, lessons about how much emotional stress my particular body is capable of handling, and lessons about human behavior.

I understand now that human behavior is an extension of the behavior of our primal animal ancestors. I saw aggression and cooperation during my days. I saw love and hate and the other thirty kinds of emotions. Biologically, we are not so much different in the kinds of behavior we emit than other mammals. We humans are different, however in how we express ourselves. It is the degree, not the kind of behavior we emit that makes us human. And when it comes to business or any other aspect of life, information is important, communication is equally, if not even more important.

Looking back now, I wouldn't trade most of my experiences in Winthrop and Okanogan County for any other. I had a wonderful time.

That time was spent around mostly wonderful people. I was part of many different kinds of functions that kept the town going and even flourishing.

By 2,000 I was back in St. Augustine, Florida, where I had once been a scientist at the Marineland Research Laboratory, where one of my favorite scientists, Dr. John Lilly (author of Man and Dolphin, Communication Between Man and Dolphin, other books, and about 50 science papers) had worked. I worked in the same laboratory where he I had worked. If I could, I was eager to find another position in science.

Unfortunately, when I arrived, I found that Marineland was no longer owned by Vanderbilt-Witney family, but by a southern family which was going to turn Marineland into something other than what it was. I couldn't land another job there.

I turned to helping people with mental and physical disabilities, and that is the profession I followed for another decade.

# Building a Home

I want to end this little book with something positive, because not everything that I have done have been such bad ideas as most of the previous stories relate, where I barely escaped with my life. The important stuff has turned out very well.

Building my own home was certainly one of my most positive experiences and one I would happily do over again. In terms of timing, it was most successful. It all started when I returned from dolphin training in Florida when my father was failing badly.

To be near him and not knowing how long he still had to live, I decided to build a house. The second day my focus was set, I found a small piece of property that a house could be set upon.

In Okanogan County, Washington, the rural areas were still mostly unregulated and there were no building codes for home builders.

I had virtually but a few dollars to my name when I decided to build. The property I bought from a local man was $1,000 and $35 a month. I figured that just working minimal hours for my father at his Last Trading Post in downtown Winthrop, I could earn my keep and the $35 a month I needed. The reason the land was so cheap was that it appeared to be land-locked and had no immediate access to a city street.

That didn't bother me, because there was an irrigation ditch running through it on one side of the property. It felt to me like a gently flowing small stream. I knew I could build a stout bridge over it, if I could find the right kind of lumber.

Fate would have it that a restaurant in the next town, Twisp, had a fallin-in roof from the previous year's snowfall. I contacted the owner and he said that if I could tear apart the roof, I could salvage the lumber and I set to work immediately.

Within a week, I had best lumber and timbers available to build my bridge, but in order to build it I had to build a wide, sloping road, connecting with the city street to even get to the area to build the bridge.

I then researched the town of Winthrop's ordinances and found out that the town had to grant me access to the street, if my property abutted the road. It did and I set out to build my road.

That small road, wide enough to drive any car down, took me about a week of hard labor. I still had lots of time and very little money, so everything worked out.

Then I set about building my bridge with my beams and stout 2" X 12" planks. That took me nearly a week since the only two tools I had to work with were a hand saw and a hammer, both borrowed from my father. I still had no electricity anywhere near my small property. That would come months later.

Ideas were coming together; so were the materials. By late fall, I had a road and a bridge, but no house to live in.

My father needed me more and more, and he paid my for my work. After all, I had a B.A. degree in Psychology by then and I could have worked for anyone in the area for a good salary. However, I couldn't get much money ahead to buy the lumber to build my house on the property.

As my luck would have it, I was working retail in the store when an old white haired man approached the register.

"Someone told me you are trying to build a house on a small piece of property," he said.

That's true," I replied.

"Okay then, I have a deal for you."

The mystery man led me to a piece of property on the other side of the Met-how River, only a half mile from my new property. If there hadn't been a bunch of 1920s farm houses in the way I could have seen his property from mine.

On his acre stood what looked like a shed. It had sliding barn doors and the small eighteen foot by twenty-eight foot building intrigued me.

It had a gently sloping tin roof and looked to have been built in the 1930s. What he said next, interested me even more.

"Here's the deal. I need this building moved or torn down and taken away in a month. I have someone interested in the property, but not the building."

"How much do you want for it. I'm working for my father and he can't afford to pay me much."

"I know all about you," the old man said with a smile. "I know you've built a road and a bridge with your bare hands. I admire that kind of spunk. Here's what I'll do." He turned away to look at the bright winter sky.

The weather was changing and it was November 15th, usually the first day of real lasting snow in the Met-how Valley. I expected it to be coming down any minute.

"I will sell you my shed and everything in it for $350."

I walked closer to the small building and noticed the sturdy brass padlock on the front.

"What's inside?" I asked him. I expected it was full of junk that I would need to cart away in order to even tear down the building. My ownly vehicle at the time was a 1967 Volkswagen bug.

"I am not telling you," the old man said. "You buy the building and the contents and I'll throw in that nice padlock."

"A pig in a polk, huh?" I joked.

"That's right. It's all or nothing and by the looks of the weather, you're going to have to take apart that building in the snow and move the lumber in the snow, too."

Everything looked so iffy that I couldn't decide right then and there, but the padlock did look like it was worth about $35.

Please, give me a couple of days to think about it," I finally said.

"Well, the buildings has sat here for forty years, so I don't suppose another couple of days will hurt," he replied.

He gave me his phone number and we went our separate ways.

It started snowing in earnest and I had a few nearly sleepless nights, trying to decide what to do. In those days, my $400 dollars was the most money I had ever been able to save at any one time and I might need it to get through the winter, especially since our store's clientele was drastically reduced, because it was tourist-oriented.

As the snow kept falling, fewer and fewer tourists came to town and to our store. By the time I decided to take a chance on the shed and its contents, there ware four feet of powder snow on the ground and more falling every minute. I called the old man.

"By when do I have to have the shed torn down and moved?" I asked.

"By February or everything that is left I will burn on the spot," the old man answered.

That sounded foreboding, but then maybe I could just dissassemble the shed and leave what might be the junk inside behind anyway. That helped me make my decision.

"Okay, I've got the $350 and I will buy your shed. I could just envision the smile on his face when he hung up the phone. He would sell his land.

We met at the property and it was still snowing. Now there was five feet of snow on the ground and I had borrowed a snow shovel from my father's store. It took me the better part of two hours to make a path from the road to the shed. He patiently watched me dig and throw, dig and throw. Soon the snow bank on either side of us was nearly eight feet tall.

"You have a lot of energy," the old man said.

I turned to look at him and took a few needed breaths.

"That's good, because you are going to need it."

I thought he was teasing me. I gave him the money and he gave me a stout steel key.

When I opened the lock and pushed aside one of the sliding barn doors I peered inside. I couldn't see to the back side of the building, but what I did see in the front of the building shocked me. The old man could have toppled me with one good breath.

Inside on wooden racks was lumber . . . thousands and thousands of feet of board lumber. There were all thicknesses of lumber, all widths of lumber and everything on the racks looked to be at least twenty feet long.

I'm sure my eyes were as round and big as softballs when I turned to see the old man smiling at me.

"Everything in here is mine?" I asked.

"You made a fine decision," said the old man. "Yes, everything on this piece of property is yours."

"My eyes started watering up, as if I was going to cry."

"How? How did you do all this?" I asked. It looked like it had been a Herculean effort at one time.

"In 1929, the Great Depression had begun. I came from Alaska with what is called an "Alaskan mill" and I decided to build my own house right here on this spot, close to the Met-how River. The A-mill is essentially a small car engine on a specially built frame. With it, you can cut logs to any size you want."

"How long did it take you to cut this wood to all these sizes?"

"About a year. All this lumber I cut from old growth fir from the area."

"I can't even begin to thank you for all this," I said. I came close and hugged him.

"You remind me a lot of me at your age," he said. "After I milled this lumber and set it on these racks to dry, I fell in love with a young lady whose family was quite well to do and I never did get around to building my house. If you don't fall in love, too, you will build your house and with this lumber. Everything you neeed is here. Inventory it. Build something nice."

It stopped snowing.

"If you need to learn how to do anything extra, here's my address."

At the time, I didn't know what he meant.

We parted company again and I went back to the Last Trading Post to tell me father. He was nearly as thrilled as I was, although he didn't believe me until he saw the shed and its contents with his own eyes.

All of a sudden, I had massive decisions to make. Where was I going to put all this beautiful forty-year-old air-dried lumber in so many sizes? How was I going to get it across the river to my property over a bridge that didn't allow anything taller than fourteen feet? How does one carry twenty-foot-long lumber on a Volkswagen bug, anyway?

After dad left to go back to the shop, I went to my property with the shovel and started shoveling again, this time to make a space in the snow to put my new, old lumber.

I dug out the snow and put it in the vacant irrigation ditch, where in the spring it would slowly dissolve and wash away down valley. That took me two days. With the rest of my money I bought big blue tarps and laid them on the ground, anchoring them with big river rocks so they wouldn't blow away.

I bought some sturdy rope, also. Then I started lashing lumber, sometimes a board at a time to the front bumper of the Volkswagen and bending it over the roof of the VW to the back bumper.

Our town marshal at the time and I grew very friendly. He, like the old man, liked ingenuity. He had never seen anyone transport lumber on a VW and we had talks about public safety and my own safety. When he saw what I was trying to deal with firsthand, he relented and wished me luck. He tried to keep out of my way after that.

As I wrote previously, there are many things that make living in small towns special. High on the list is the people who live in them. It is so important for people to work together, even if it is to the benefit of a single person. What comes around goes around and you never know when you will need another person's help. Without the old man and our friendly marshal, I never would have built that house.

For nearly a month. I made multi-daily trips back and forth across the river with lumber. Each time I dropped it off at my property, I made a record of the amount, length and width of the wood I transported. Finally, all the lumber was out of the shed and I had an inventory.

Next came the even harder part. I had to take apart the shed itself. December was a particularly snowy month. I borrowed a heavy iron nail puller and began taking the shed apart, the nail puller in one hand and a hammer in the other. Surprisingly, they worked well together on the long, sturdy nails that held the wonderfully weathered and colorful "barn wood" to its heavy two-by-four studs. I saved and straightened every nail for future use.

In another month through the snow and cold, I had torn down the shed and transported it to my property under the tarps that was already covering the prime lumber.

By and by, I met my deadline. The old man's property was cleared of a shed, its contents, and all the nails that had once covered the grounds during the dissassembly. I was joyful.

I met a really fine woman and things turned out differently for me than for the old man. She wasn't rich, but she was a good worker, and in my mind that accounts for a lot. During that winter, she got a job working for Sun Mountain Lodge. I moved in with her. She supported me while I drew up the blue prints for our house that I would build in the spring.

When I was going to the University of Washington, one of my friends was becoming an architect and since I also love architecture, I would drop in on his classes from time to time. That's how I learned about blue-prints. Mine, however, weren't blue. They were just white, and on sheets of typing paper fastened to each other. As I said, in those days, there weren't building codes, so having real blue prints wasn't necessary. My plans, however, were as finely detailed as blueprints and because of my inventory, I knew exactly what my new house on the irrigation ditch would look like.

In the early spring after some of the snow had melted, I started digging around the lumber until I had dug a basement. With river rocks from the Met-how River and with mortar I made from cement and lime, I constructed basement walls. When that was done, I built the first floor of solid timbers and thick boards. If I had wanted to, I could have trained elephants on that first floor.

One day, a person stopped by and gave me a brand new box of tenpenny nails. Another person gave me a half box of small-headed finish nails. And so it went . . . as the building rose off the ground, neighbors got involved. One brought me lunch occasionally, another brought a window.

The framework of the building grew to three stories tall by the middle of April. It was still just me and my hammer and saw; still no electricity.

I couldn't afford the power pole and the 200 amp box I would need. Besides, I wouldn't be living in the house until it at least had some walls.

My father had been watching the building going up with some pride. He hadn't ever attemtped doing something like it and he offered to buy me the plywood I needed for the siding of the tall house. I couldn't turn him down.

By early June, the building had walls. Now all I needed was windows and doors. I couldn't afford them, either.

An old lady came to me one day as I was hammering the roof plywood down. She motioned for me to come down. I did.

"I own a house that was built about 1910 and it has had some severe snow damage over the years. I live in Seattle now, but I heard through the local grapevine that you need some windows."

"Whoever you got the information from, thank them for me, because windows and doors are my next step. Thank you, too. At this point, I don't even care what they look like."

She wrote me a permission note so that if anyone saw me tearing out the windows from her old building, they wouldn't have grounds to call the police. I never saw her again.

I immediately rushed to her old homestead. She was the old woman the old man had been married to. After fifty years, she had decided the winter snows were too much for her. The old man had decided to continue to live in the Met-how.

I called him to make sure the windows were still mine.

"It's always been her house to do with what she pleases," said the old man. "It isn't worth living in anymore . . . too much damage at too high a cost to fix. I live in another house. Have at it, young man. How is your house coming?"

"Thanks to you, it's three stories high and is looking to be everything I ever wanted to live in."

"I'm so pleased you are living your dream," he said. Not many people do." He hung up the landline phone.

By mid-June all the windows were in. Now I needed a front and a rear door. Old ones were all over the valley, but for some reason, I wanted something special.

One day a very special friend came by. He was the one I had hiked into Lost Lakes and nearly into Devil's Canyon with. He said he was making stained glass works. I asked him if he could make me a couple of doors.

"I could try," he said. "So far I've only been making lamps and windows."

"I'll pay for you to try," I said.

By late June, the tourist season was well underway and my father had been making more and more use of me as his health failed. He also wanted to spend some of his last days with his youngest sons from his Icelandic family. I concurred. Everything was working together. I was paying off my siding and making enough extra money to pay for the doors.

When they came, a couple weeks later, I was thrilled. They were beautiful and added a lot to the house. There was only one thing missing on the house—a chimney. In winter, it gets below zero in the Met-how Valley. That's why the snow is soft and fluffy and generally easy to shovel.

While I was thinking about how to build a chimney, another elderly man I had never met came into the Last Trading Post.

He said, "I am dying of cancer . . . I smoked like a chimney for years (I think that was a joke), but I hear you want to build a chimney for your new house and I'm your man."

Now, how do you turn down someone like that? I couldn't.

I got my first credit card and charged a dozen cement blocks, a bag of concrete, and a bag of lime to it and hauled them in my well-used VW to the house site.

When he arrived he said, "You're going to need lots more of everything, because you're going to build the best God-damned chimney in the whole valley. It's going to be a monument to me."

That sounded really awesome and a bit overwhelming to a person who had never built anything but river rock basement walls.

He looked up at the tall house. "If It's going to work here on this house, it's got to be a double chimney at least thirty-five feet tall."

All I could say was, "Wow!"

"Let's get started." He wheeled his wheelbarrow from his truck down my road and over my bridge. He cut open both the cement bag and the lime bag and poured them into the wheelbarrow. Then he instructed me to get water from the irrigation ditch and mix up the materials.

He laid two of the chimney blocks side by side and after I had thoroughly mixed the components, he applied the slather between the blocks and on top of them. Then he added two blocks on top of them.

"Now . . . go buy some red tile liners. They go in next, before we add too many chimney blocks. They have to go up together . . . chimney blocks . . . liners . . . chimney blocks . . . liners . . . like that."

After I gathered everything he told me, he started making a couple more rows. "I hope you've been watching me closely," he said, "because you're doing the rest . . . all the way to the top."

"Me?" I was somewhat dumbfounded.

"Yes, you. My health won't permit me go any higher."

I asked myself silently, "What am I getting myself into this time?" As I got higher off the ground, I would need to build scaffolding of some sort.

Somehow he knew what I was thinking. He said, "My brother has scaffolding. He'll let you use it for awhile. This chimney shouldn't take you more than a couple of weeks."

When a person focuses on something s(he) sincerely wants to do, it seems that the whole universe opens up and helps to make it happen. At least, it did for me in the great, small town of Winthrop. The communication grapevine did its best and people came from all parts of the valley to make my dream come true.

My girlfriend and I remained together in that wonderful house for twenty-nine years. It never caused us one problem, one concern. Nothing except a water heater ever broke down and needed repair. (We actually went through two brand new water heaters.)

The VW that had carried all that wood across the river carried she and I on two great trips to Mexico and back and on another great trip to the Florida Keys and back. We retired it and it sits comfortably basking in the sun on another property we owned together, overlooking the North Cascade Mountains.

About a year before my father died, I bought the Last Trading Post from him and over the years divided the sale price between the brothers of his two families. My partner and I ran that terrific establishment all during the time we lived in our wonderful house by the irrigation ditch. It still stands. Unfortunately, the Last Trading Post doesn't. It burned down on Christmas day about ten years after I sold the business of a young married couple who ran it that decade.

# Falls

The older one gets, the more often one gets to visit a doctor's office or a hospital. These days, I take care of three other people, all a bit younger than me who have different kinds of health problems. None of them drive anymore so that is but one of the conveniences I provide for them. Doctor's visits, medication runs, food runs to various kinds of establishments are more kinds of free services that I provide for these three, and for myself.

My health is pretty stable. I take no medication except for an occasional aspirin or a sleeping pill on those nights when I'm totally keyed up by television politics or some form of gambling, which I sometimes enjoy. When I take one of my clients to a doctor's office, I generally have a baleful of questions to ask his or her doctor. Thankfully, these questions get answers and I can afterward attend even closer to the needs of my clients.

One of the useful things I've learned about aging is that one or both of two things will eventually kill an elder person. One is pneumonia; the other is falls of one sort or another. I've never had pneumonia, although I think I've probably come close enough during bouts of hypothermia. I have, however, now experienced different kinds of falls, a couple of which could easily have killed me if I had landed the wrong way. I've related my motorcycle crash that sent me sprawling. I also flew off a highbar while doing an Eagle while I was a gymnast at the University of Washington. I dislocated a shoulder. An then there was the episode of falling from 32 feet while I was disassembling that antique barn. I dislocated the same left shoulder. At my current age, there is arthritis in that shoulder now, but I only feel it when the weather drastically changes. I can still type on my computer keyboard as I am doing presently.

Another fall I had was actually my worst and it was the most stupid of all of them. I was holding a can of pop while going from an all-night grocery outlet. My car was on the other side of a curb. I slipped on the curb and literally broke my neck. My neck swelled up and I couldn't get off the ground. I was in honest-to-goodness pain. I scratched around for my cell-phone and called 911. At the time, no-one else was around despite my yelling at the top of my lungs. The ambulance finally arrived and the EMTs positioned my neck in a brace and hauled me off. I felt every bump in the road on the way to the hospital. That's how bad was the pain. After they placed me in the MRI, the technician discovered the swollen neck and that a piece of my spine had broken off and would forever lodge in my neck like a piece of war scrapnel.

Whenever I turn my neck these days, I can feel it. If I don't do something very foolish so that the little piece doesn't attack my spinal cord nerves or a major blood vessel, I'll keep on living a normal life.

But then one never knows what the devil will happen in the next few day, months, years...

One fine fall day, I was helping a woman client of my mine navigate the front stairs to our rented house. She slipped and the belt I was holding onto, a tough medical belt, held so that I more or less gently lowered her to the cement ground around the staircase. However, the angle I was at motioned me right through the staircase and onto the ground. I broke several boards that I landed on. Nails protruded everywhere. I felt for broken bones, that broken piece in my neck, and elsewhere looking for any problem. Fortunately, I escaped major injury and so did the lady. We were both very lucky.

She had previously broken her hip so a fall of any kind could have been disastrous. And for me, as well, considering my broken neck.

As of this writing, I now watch for cracks in sidewalks, curbs, unusual rises and fallings of earth in yards, and am generally completely conscious of my surroundings wherever I go. I've had a good life and I'd like to see it extended even a bit more.

# Epilogue

Some things happen by misfortune; some things happen by pure accident; some things happen for a reason. I have experienced some form of all of these.

If I had it to do all over again from a pick of lots of different possibilities, I would pick my life to do all over again, given the same outcomes. I would skip traveling the freeway in the wrong direction, however. That was just plain stupid and other people who have done it have died horribly.

One of the joys of getting old and still retaining an alert mind is that you can relate your passions and experiences to others. This I have done through these true tales. I hope you have learned a thing or two after reading them.

One more thing: Despite the many failings of our society, we are very lucky to be living in these times. There are so many different kinds of help a person can receive these days with the simple press of a few buttons. At Central Washington University, I worked on a Crisis Hotline. Over land-line phones at the time, I heard all manner of problems that affect young people trying to achieve academically. Drug addictions, issues relating to love affairs gone sour, gambling problems, terrible tests, teachers who seem to hate their students, and so on. A friendly voice on a line can help prevent a suicide. Simple guidance, sometimes, can prevent a drug overdose; parnerships can halt alcholism, and so forth. We are all lucky that these kinds of interventions, and many others, are available to each and every person who is stuck in a jam and reaches out for help. My best advice to young folks, therefore, is to seek the help you feel you need to solve whatever problem set is plaguing you.

Auguste Rodin, the great French sculptor, created The Thinker on the cover of this book as an athlete, thinking. He knew that thinking was a powerful exercise. Employ it always in your endeavors and remember my motto: NEVER DIE YOUNG.

www.ingramcontent.com/pod-product-compliance
Lightning Source LLC
Chambersburg PA
CBHW022009120526
44592CB00034B/750